Traumas and Suicide
Prevention

For Warriors by Warriors

Charles "Chuck" Wright

Copyright © 2021 Charles "Chuck" Wright
All rights reserved
First Edition

Fulton Books, Inc.
Meadville, PA

Published by Fulton Books 2021

ISBN 978-1-64952-708-0 (paperback)
ISBN 978-1-64952-753-0 (hardcover)
ISBN 978-1-64952-709-7 (digital)

Printed in the United States of America

Disclaimer Statement

This Guidebook could help anyone when they feel that, there is no reason to live or no reason for life. The contributors and writers that have shared their testimonies in our Guidebook do not encourage traumas or suicide, nor encourage harm to others, in the past, present, or future.

Contents

Our Mission Statement 7
Introduction 9
Foreword 11
Book on Stories of Overcoming PTSD, Depression,
    Loss, Anger, Suicidal Ideations, Panic Disorders 15
How it all Began – Charles Chuck Wright 19
Acknowledgments 21
PTSD Basics 23
Volunteering as Therapy – Chap 1950 29
One Quiet Day at Church – Charles Chuck Wright 32
My Time in Vietnam – George Howe 35
The Four Elements to My Recovery – Joe Sturdevant 37
Duc Lap, Vietnam 1968 – Jon C. Bartine 46
Kon Tum – Jon C. Bartine 52
The Saga of Bent Bent Four – Jon C. Bartine 63
HELP Is on the Way! "STRESSORS" – W.S. "Stan" Wright 73
One Day at a Time – W.S. "Stan" Wright 77
Anxiety 84
From Teenager to Manhood in Less Than a Year –
    John Young 88
Bubba Bowie – Michael Hunt 90
Like Fleas on a Hound Dog – Willie Spurlin 94
No One Heals Alone – Joshua Clark 96
Self-Care and Coping with PTSD Effects 101
Grateful for My Comrades – Ron "Rabbit" Clark 110
Observations on My Vietnam Experience – Delta 56 112

Understanding and Coping with My Mental
    Challenges – Jesus I. Olivo 117
My PTSD Story – Ross R. Read, MBA 119
Personal Health and Well-Being 124
Reach Out to be Heard – Robert Garcia............................. 131
Propelled for Purpose – Hannah Clark 134
How Forgiveness and Gratitude Transformed My
    Life – Jo Ann Rotermund.. 138
The Trauma of Losing a Child – J. Bennett....................... 143
My Beautiful Blue-Eyed Christopher – Sandy Gambill...... 153
Dealing with Sadness or Grief after a Loss 158
I Am No One – Allison T. 163
How I Went from Desperately Wanting to Kill
    Myself to Loving Every Minute of My Life –
    Sondi Jones 166
Keeping Your Children Alive and Happy Through
    Their School Years – J. Adams..................................... 173
Military Sexual Trauma 177
What is Moral Injury? 183
Learning War and Reconciliation – Rev. David Peters 188
Reconciliation – Rev. George McGavern 195
Helpful Organizations, Websites, and Reference Materials 201

Our Mission Statement

Traumas and Suicide Prevention for Warriors by Warriors is committed to helping others overcome their traumas and suicidal actions by improving their lives in any way possible with the help of our Lord, our families, our friends, and others that are so committed "in His Service".

Introduction

Charles "Chuck" Wright
Author and Founder

Richard Dorn
Editor

The collection of testimonies you are going to read contains the real stories that were written and submitted by each of the courageous men and women. Some are ordinary people who experienced extraordinary traumas and loss. Others are stories of veterans who served in conflicts from Vietnam, the Gulf War, Iraq, and Afghanistan. The common denominator in these testimonies is trauma which does not distinguish between military or civilian. Many of the stories describe thoughts of doing personal harm or harm to others. They describe their struggling with alcohol and drugs and drawing into cocoons of solitude. The common link in each story is endurance and survival and how they returned to a less tumultuous and difficult existence. Resources are in the book to aid veterans, families, caregivers, spouses, and others suffering from the effects of trauma in ways to get help. It is our greatest wish that this book will provide hope to endure for those who are suffering. Use this as your guidebook to help overcome your stressors.

Foreword

This collection of testimonies from both veterans and nonveterans alike shares personal reflections on very difficult times in each of their lives when violent and traumatic experiences changed them forever. We hope it gives our readers insight on how our contributors survived these most difficult times and gives hope to those suffering the consequences of post-traumatic stress disorder (PTSD) and moral injury.

PTSD has been widely discussed in our culture over many decades, particularly after Vietnam. The term PTSD is relatively new; however, the aftermath and symptoms are not. Literature, going back hundreds of years, has revealed traumatic experiences and the symptom's effects on their characters' lives.

Our country's history has long recognized the psychological effects of trauma and terminology evolved as the medical community learned more about the aftereffects upon veterans. In the mid to late 19th century, the term "nostalgia" was embraced to describe soldiers experiencing mental trauma such as sadness, homesickness, sleep problems, and anxiety. This became the model of psychological trauma in the Civil War.

With the advent of World War I, "shell shock" became the term adopted to describe the effects constant artillery bombardment had on soldiers. It was believed that brain damage resulted from shelling. Panic and sleep problems were widely recorded among soldiers being treated. Thinking changed when more soldiers who were not experienced to shelling were also having the same symptoms, which then described as "war neuroses."

During World War II, shell shock was replaced with the term "battle fatigue." Exhausted soldiers were constantly on the go and fighting in unimaginable conditions which took an inevitable toll on them. Many of our military commanders did not recognize battle fatigue as a real problem, General George Patton being prominent among them.

The present-day terminology of PTSD came to existence in 1980 when the American Psychiatric Association (APA) added this to the Diagnostic and Statistical Manual of Mental Disorders (DSM). The inclusion of this term resulted from studies involving returned Vietnam veterans and others. The links between war trauma and the trauma survivors was finally established.

Moral injury is closely intertwined but distinct from PTSD. The Moral Injury Project at Syracuse University describes it as follows:

> Moral injury is the damage done to one's conscience or moral compass when that person perpetrates, witnesses, or fails to prevent acts that transgress one's own moral beliefs, values, or ethical codes of conduct.

Moral injury is not new as a concept. Basically it is as old as war itself. Literature and history have many recorded instances of moral injury and the ethical dilemmas which our warriors experienced and endured. Examples of moral injury in wartime are typically:

- using deadly force in combat and causing the harm or death of civilians knowingly but without alternatives or accidentally;
- giving orders in combat that result in the injury or death of a fellow service member;
- failing to provide medical aid to an injured civilian or service member;
- returning home from deployment and hearing of the executions of cooperating local nationals;

- failing to report knowledge of a sexual assault or rape committed against oneself, a fellow service member, or civilians;
- following orders that were illegal, immoral, and against the rules of engagement (ROE) or Geneva convention; and
- a change in belief about the necessity or justification for war during or after one's service.

Coping with moral injury is challenging because of its profound and deep effects on those who experienced it. Moral injury must be recognized across our nation, and caregivers need to be aware of its effects. Communities are encouraged to listen and encourage those suffering from moral injury. Numerous avenues are available to aid in comforting and confronting moral injury victims. Common therapies and activities can include art, writing or journaling, religious dialogue, and peer discussion groups as examples. Further discussion follows in this guidebook. As we go forward, *it's okay to not be okay!*

Richard Dorn
Editor

Sources:

Friedman, Matthew. "History of PTSD in Veterans: Civil War to DSM-5." https://www.ptsd.va.gov/understand/what/history_ptsd.asp

Puniewska, Maggie. "Healing a Wounded Sense of Morality." July 3, 2015. https://www.theatlantic.com/health/archive/2015/07/healing-a-wounded-sense-of-morality/396770/

Syracuse University. "What is Moral Injury." http://moralinjuryproject.syr.edu/about-moral-injury/

Book on Stories of Overcoming PTSD, Depression, Loss, Anger, Suicidal Ideations, Panic Disorders

Introductory Comments

The book whose introduction you are now reading contains the real stories of men and women who faced a myriad of physical, emotional, and relational traumas and difficulties. Some were ordinary people who endured extraordinary trials, tribulation, and loss. Others are unsung heroes of various battles waged in remote locations around the world or within themselves or their families or friends. Still others are average people whose average problems simply became overwhelming to them at some point.

The reality is all people experience difficulties and have done so for as long as there have been people. Everyone experiences difficulties, distractions, diseases, and disasters that threaten to undo them. The difficulties may be physical, mental, emotional, cultural, geopolitical, or spiritual. What is likely more common is that it is a combination of some, or all, of the factors just mentioned. Such struggles then spill over into relationships with parents, partners, friends, family, and fellow workers, or even human society itself. What is interesting and worth pondering is that since suffering and struggling seems to be everyone's experience, where in the world did we develop such a broadly held belief? Some would argue that this expectation is just a bunch of fairy tale beliefs, but its pervasiveness among the human family would argue for something more pervasive and powerful.

In some cases, you may soon read the stresses and strains that came upon those telling their stories that brought them to a desperate and dark consideration of harming themselves or others. For others, the pain and perplexities led to seeking to silence the thoughts and feelings screaming within them through self-medication with alcohol, prescription medication, illicit drugs, or an unbridled pursuit of pleasure or distraction. Still others withdrew into a silent, empty cocoon of solitude. The common thread in each of the stories to come is one of endurance and survival that lead to the discovery of some different line of thinking, feeling, or relating that then brought about a return to a less tumultuous and difficult place. Some of the stories will bring emotional or spiritual help to bear. Others will describe simpler and less complicated help to bear.

The common thread here is that we all have and will struggle with similar questions about the confusion and chaos in life: "Why do good things happen to bad people and bad things happen to good people?" "Why did this happen to me?" or "What did I do or not do to deserve this?" to name just a few. If we are honest enough to admit thinking these or other questions like them, it can similarly return us to what a friend of my mine struggling with a disease that gradually rendered him incapable of thought or action once said to my wife and me. Someone had asked him simply, "Why do you think this is happening to you?" His response was simply to say, "It is more helpful for me to ponder why shouldn't this happen to me since it happens to others struggling too." Clearly thinking in both directions is worth at least some consideration before we assign ourselves to blame, shame, or despair. Should we simply resolve ourselves to the mess that lead us to pick up this book or others who are like it?

I am a pastor at a church who believes that we are all residents on the fictional Island of Misfit Toys, struggling with things that keep us off-balance and out of synch with ourselves, others, our context and culture, and ultimately with God too. But we do not believe it is not our job to fix people. The Bible itself shows just how easy it is for people who are trying to help others to do more harm than good! We also do not take stock in denying our own inability to do very well at fixing ourselves. But we also believe that when we have a community that is characterized by goodness, generosity, and grace, environment provides the catalyst we need for change. When that starts occurring, we soon realize we are better together than we are as individuals. In short, we are made to live in a healthy and vibrant community of care, concern, and acceptance. It is there that help, hope, and healing occur over time.

This is not a book written by ivory-tower scholars sitting who pontificate powerless platitudes that end up hurting more than helping. The stories are real people telling their stories with the hope that something in that story—something that may have taken them years or decades to discover and practice—actually started helping. Because it helped them, they hope it will help you, too, and perhaps more rapidly and less painfully than it was for them. If that does occur and something one of the contributors has offered helps you, please repeat the favor and choose to do the same thing. Join a support group and look and listen for opportunities to share after you ask and receive permission to do so. Then keep in touch so you can encourage, coach, or keep growing yourself. The goal is to bring real hope and help to real people struggling with real problems because someone also helped each of us along the way. Each contributor to this work is doing for you what someone else is doing in a support group, over a meal with a friend, by simply by being there with someone who was or is hurting to support and sustain them during dark and difficult times. Help and hope come best where there is truth, mutually beneficial relationships, and a community that focuses on helping others, not just helping themselves, as we believe you may hear and see in the stories that follow.

With hope for real help,
Bill Himmel
Associate Pastor, Restoration
Real Life Ministries
Tomball, Texas

How It All Began

Greetings to our readers and supporters.

This undertaking began in the spring of 2019. I was serving as the acting facilitator of 23 combat warriors who met weekly. In our group, we couldn't help but talk about the number of veterans committing suicide on a daily basis. At that time, the number was in the low 20's, but within a few weeks, the number rose to 26 and was still climbing for a while.

Several weeks later in one of our meetings, one of the vets stood up and said, "Enough is enough. We need to do something." That was all it took for everyone to have a different solution. Before our session ended, we had two different ways to help our vets. We voted and had a name for our project. It was going to be Ways to Prevent Veteran Suicide from A to Z.

A few weeks passed before we met again. The men collectively wanted to tell others how they overcame the urge to commit suicide and how they handled the stressors instead of taking their own life. Someone suggested it could be called Your Guidebook Through Stressors. But finally the name was born: Traumas and Suicide Prevention for Warriors by Warriors. We have built a website, www.stpwarriors.org, which is under construction and will be finished in the very near future.

So with some initial testimonies… "Traumas and Suicide Prevention for Warriors by Warriors" Guidebook was born. **The book is meant to help others find solutions to preserve their lives when at times there seems to be no other way except to take one's life.** Military testimonies started coming in from a few veterans. Almost everyone whom I spoke with wanted to help their fellow veteran. One veteran said, "If it helps to save one life then it's worth it."

Nonmilitary men and woman who suffered traumas also wanted to share their testimonies, so we included their stories to be a part of this undertaking. Stress is stress, be it veteran or civilian. At that time, we realized that others who did not serve in the military did serve in their own way with families, their community, church, school, etc. They coped with their own stressors daily.

Some of the contributors requested anonymity and will be identified by pseudonyms to respect their privacy. Many shared, for the very first time, stories never discussed and wrote about their innermost thoughts and reflections on their traumas. We recognize that perhaps some of our readers may wish to contract an author or the author wishes to respond to a reader. Those requests will be handed in a professional and confidential manner. Please contact me by e-mail, starshipbc.charles1@gmail.com, so that we can facilitate any requests or questions that may arise.

Our deepest thanks to each one of you, our readers and supporters. You can also make a difference. Show and tell your family and friends that you care and that *you love them* 24/7.

Semper fidelis!
Charles "Chuck" Wright
Author and Founder

Acknowledgments

This book is dedicated to the ones who have given their testimonies within our book for us to share with our fellow warriors, military, and civilian men and women. There were others who shared their stressors within our combat peer support group who met weekly at our VA outpatient clinic in Tomball, Texas.

Each person in our group gave a personal oath that what we shared in our group stayed in our group. It is with a great personal commitment that I've shared several times over the past five-plus years that I trust each man as though my life depended on them now and forever. Each man has made a difference in my life.

A thank you goes to the clergy whom we have come to know as this book went forward, specifically the ministers and staff at Real Life Church in Tomball, Texas; Good Shepherd Episcopal Church in Tomball, Texas; and the Episcopal Veterans Fellowship in Austin, Texas. Their assistance and prayers are gratefully appreciated.

"Greater love has no one than this, that one lay down his life for his friends" (John 15:13, American Standard Bible The Open Bible Edition).

Charles "Chuck" Wright
Author and Founder

Be gentle with yourself, you're doing the best you can.

PTSD Basics

Available in Spanish (https://www.ptsd.va.gov/spanish/ptsd_basics_sp.asp)

PTSD (post-traumatic stress disorder) is a mental health problem that some people develop after experiencing or witnessing a life-threatening event, like combat, a natural disaster, a car accident, or sexual assault.

It's normal to have upsetting memories, to feel on edge, or to have trouble sleeping after a traumatic event. At first, it may be hard to do normal daily activities, like go to work, go to school, or spend time with people you care about. But most people start to feel better after a few weeks or months.

If it's been longer than a few months and you're still having symptoms, you may have PTSD. For some people, PTSD symptoms may start later on, or they may come and go over time.

Who Develops PTSD?

Anyone can develop PTSD at any age. A number of factors can increase the chance that someone will have PTSD, many of which are not under that person's control. For example, having a very intense or long-lasting traumatic event or getting injured during the event can make it more likely that a person will develop PTSD. PTSD is also more common after certain types of trauma, like combat and sexual assault.

Personal factors, like previous traumatic exposure, age, and gender, can affect whether or not a person will develop PTSD.

What happens after the traumatic event is also important. Stress can make PTSD more likely while social support can make it less likely.

What Are the Symptoms of PTSD?

PTSD symptoms usually start soon after the traumatic event, but they may not appear until months or years later. They also may come and go over many years. If the symptoms last longer than four weeks, cause you great distress, or interfere with your work or home life, you might have PTSD.

There are four types of PTSD symptoms, but they may not be exactly the same for everyone. Each person experiences symptoms in their own way.

1. Reliving the event (also called reexperiencing symptoms). Memories of the traumatic event can come back at any time. You may feel the same fear and horror you did when the event took place. For example:

   o You may have nightmares.
   o You may feel like you are going through the event again. (This is called a flashback.)
   o You may see, hear, or smell something that causes you to relive the event. This is called a trigger. News reports, seeing an accident, or hearing a car backfire are examples of triggers.

2. Avoiding situations that remind you of the event. You may try to avoid situations or people that trigger

memories of the traumatic event. You may even avoid talking or thinking about the event. For example:

- o You may avoid crowds because they feel dangerous.
- o You may avoid driving if you were in a car accident or if your military convoy was bombed.
- o If you were in an earthquake, you may avoid watching movies about earthquakes.
- o You may keep very busy or avoid seeking help because it keeps you from having to think or talk about the event.

3. Negative changes in beliefs and feelings. The way you think about yourself and others changes because of the trauma. This symptom has many aspects, including the following:

- o You may not have positive or loving feelings toward other people and may stay away from relationships.
- o You may forget about parts of the traumatic event or not be able to talk about them.
- o You may think the world is completely dangerous and no one can be trusted.

4. Feeling keyed up (also called hyperarousal). You may be jittery or always alert and on the lookout for danger. You might suddenly become angry or irritable. This is known as hyperarousal. For example:

- o You may have a hard time sleeping.
- o You may have trouble concentrating.

- o You may be startled by a loud noise or surprise.
- o You might want to have your back to a wall in a restaurant or waiting room.

What Are the Symptoms of PTSD in Children?

Children may have symptoms described above or other symptoms depending on how old they are. As children get older, their symptoms are more like those of adults. Here are some examples of PTSD symptoms in children:

- Children under 6 may get upset if their parents are not close by, have trouble sleeping, or act out the trauma through play.
- Children ages 7 to 11 may also act out the trauma through play, drawings, or stories. Some have nightmares or become more irritable or aggressive. They may also want to avoid school or have trouble with schoolwork or friends.
- Children age 12 to 18 have symptoms more similar to adults: depression, anxiety, withdrawal, or reckless behavior like substance abuse or running away.

Read more about PTSD in children and teens, and very young trauma survivors in the following sites:

- https://www.ptsd.va.gov/understand/what/teens_ptsd.asp
- https://www.ptsd.va.gov/understand/what/young_trauma_survivors.asp

Will People with PTSD Get Better?

After a traumatic event, it's normal to think, act, and feel differently than usual, but most people start to feel better after a few weeks or months. Talk to a doctor or mental health care provider (like a psychiatrist, psychologist, or social worker) if your symptoms last longer than a few months, are very upsetting, and disrupt your daily life.

"Getting better" means different things for different people. There are many different treatment options for PTSD. For many people, these treatments can get rid of symptoms altogether. Others find they have fewer symptoms or feel that their symptoms are less intense. Your symptoms don't have to interfere with your everyday activities, work, and relationships.

What Treatments Are Available?

There are two main types of treatment: psychotherapy (sometimes called counseling or talk therapy) and medication. Sometimes people combine psychotherapy and medication.

Psychotherapy for PTSD

Psychotherapy, or counseling, involves meeting with a therapist.

Trauma-focused psychotherapy, which focuses on the memory of the traumatic event or its meaning, is the most effective treatment for PTSD. There are different types of trauma-focused psychotherapy, such as:

- Cognitive Processing Therapy (CPT) where you learn skills to understand how trauma changed your

thoughts and feelings. Changing how you think about the trauma can change how you feel,
- Prolonged Exposure (PE) where you talk about your trauma repeatedly until memories are no longer upsetting. This will help you get more control over your thoughts and feelings about the trauma. You also go to places or do things that are safe but that you have been staying away from because they remind you of the trauma, and
- Eye Movement Desensitization and Reprocessing (EMDR), which involves focusing on sounds or hand movements while you talk about the trauma. This helps your brain work through the traumatic memories.

Medications for PTSD

Medications can be effective too. Some specific SSRIs (selective serotonin reuptake inhibitors) and SNRIs (serotonin-norepinephrine reuptake inhibitors), which are used for depression, also work for PTSD. These include sertraline, paroxetine, fluoxetine, and venlafaxine. Your mental health and medical care providers can provide specific information if they determine medication is suggested.

Source: PTSD: National Center for PTSD. https://www.ptsd.va.gov

Volunteering as Therapy

"Chap 1950"

I grew up in a time when I had very little rights as a young Black man, but that didn't stop me from having dreams for my life. I wanted to go to college and get a good education. I was eighteen years old and had recently graduated from high school. I planned to enlist in the Navy, serve my country for a few years, and then pursue my college education. Unfortunately, when I tried to enlist in the navy, I was denied for medical reasons.

About three months after being denied, my mother called me and told me I had received a letter from the government at her house.

"It looks important," she said.

"Well go ahead and open it if it looks important," I told her.

She read the letter to me. "The Army. You're being drafted."

I couldn't believe it. I didn't understand how I could be denied by the Navy but get drafted by the Army in a matter of months. I reported to the customs house in Opelousas, Louisiana.

"Why am I being drafted after being denied by the Navy?" I asked after arriving at the customs house.

I never got a straight answer. The only thing I was told was that I didn't have to retake any of the tests or do another physical since I already had done that with the Navy.

I was told to report to New Orleans that day, so my mom drove me to the bus station. She was not acting like herself during the car ride. She knew there was a war going on, and she did not want me to leave. She started tearing up when we got to the bus station. "Mom, I'll be alright. I'll call you later on," I assured her before I boarded the bus. When I got to my seat, I realized I didn't have a window seat, so I wasn't able to see my mom as the bus drove away. After arriving in New Orleans, I walked to the convenience store and got a bunch of change so I could keep in touch with her by telephone. We shipped out that same night.

I remember it was March 1970 at midnight when we headed to Fort Polk, Louisiana. It was there that I completed my six-week basic training followed by six weeks of Advanced Individual Training (AIT). My MOS was 36K20, communications. After AIT, I got my orders for Vietnam. I had one week before heading to 'Nam, and I went home to say goodbye to my family and friends. It hadn't hit me yet that I was headed for war. After that week was up, I made it to Seattle and stayed there for a week getting all new gear then boarded a big ragged plane call a Flying Tiger. I ended up in Bien Hoa for a few days, and then I left for Phu Loi to meet up with 2nd Field Force, Artillery.

When I got there, I found out that I was only attached to 2nd Field Force. My boss was a warrant officer with the cavalry. After 1 week of in-country training, I was shipped out to a firebase called Snuffy. That's when it set in that this was no place to be. It was raining all day and night, 155mm and 175mm big guns firing all day and night, incoming rounds of fire coming right back at us, mostly around mess time. After going on a few turkey shoot missions, I knew my life was in danger.

After one year of traveling place to place, setting up firebases, I finally got to go home for a week. But nothing was the same, so I went AWOL for another 26 days to try and get my head together. It didn't work. My life was a mess. All my dreams had gone out of the window. I no longer wanted to go to college, as I once had. I turned to alcohol and isolation. I had constant anxiety and nightmares. I didn't like being around crowded places, loud people, and wooded areas. I went from job to job until I became a truck driver, and that became my job of choice for the last 37 years. I'm better off as a private person.

After I was forced to retire, the only thing that helps me today with my PTSD is volunteering at the VA hospital as much as I possibly can. I volunteer in the hospice ward, helping with the No Veteran Dies Alone program. It gives me peace of mind and is the best therapy I've ever had being there for my brothers and sisters in their last days.

One Quiet Day at Church

Charles "Chuck" Wright

For 15, 25, 35+ years after I returned from Vietnam, I was told by my family and friends that my experiences in the Marines should be in my past. My memories of serving as a Marine in Vietnam were so vivid that "just moving on" wasn't possible for me.

I remember during my 8 weeks in boot camp, our drill instructor told us, "Pay attention and do not fall asleep, for it might cost you your life. If you are ever on perimeter guard duty during the night, the Vietcong can sneak up behind you and slip a piano wire around your neck and you'll be dead within seconds." This fear stuck in the back of my mind.

Fast forward 18 years later and I'm sitting in church with my wife. We were sitting in the middle section of the sanctuary with friends in front of us and to the left and right side of us. Behind us, there sat some teenage girls chattering. In retrospect, I let my guard down because I always make a point to sit closest to an exit without my back to the door. During the sermon, I was following the preacher as he read scriptures from his Bible. I heard the girls behind us get up and leave, but I did not hear them when they came back. One of the girls brushed the back of my neck. "The Vietcong can sneak up behind you and slip a piano wire around your neck and you'll be dead within seconds." Without thinking, I shut my Bible, jumped up, and turned around, ready to kill the enemy. I stood over the girl for several minutes, it seemed. I can still recall the girl's eyes, wide open and full of fear. Seeing the fear in her eyes was what snapped my mind back to reality. I ran out of the sanctuary in tears, knowing I had almost taken someone's life to save myself from the piano wire I was warned about 18 years earlier.

After the service, my wife finally found me. I was hiding under a table in a Sunday School classroom, scared and frightened that I could have hurt the girl. In that traumatic moment, I needed comfort. I needed my wife to get under the table with me and hug me. "Everybody is gone. Let's go home," she said matter-of-factly. I came out from under the table, and I was still looking around, embarrassed from what I had done and on guard about what might happen. Everyone was gone, and the parking lot was empty of cars. My wife drove us home. As we were going home, she asked me, "Do you want to call the girl and apologize?" Shocked, I said, "No, you call the girl's mother and just tell her to tell her daughter that I had a flashback from my tour in Vietnam."

That afternoon, after having lunch with my family, I told them that I needed some time to think. We had some leftover bread at the house, so I went to feed the ducks out at the lake. Taking a long walk and getting away from everybody did help, but I couldn't forget the look on the teenage girl's face when I was about to attack her. Even though I was back from Vietnam, I still had the attitude of "kill or be killed." I cried, knowing that I could take someone's life without giving it a second thought. I remember those ducks going after the bread without a worry or a fear in their little bodies. Why can't my life be like those ducks?

The crying never stopped each time I thought about my fellow combat Marines and the carnage and ugliness of the war. I still think it was such a waste of mankind and know now that it was the downfall of my marriage. With time and a lot of help from our Lord, some 40+ years after returning from "hell," the crying that I could not stop…stopped at the drop of a hat.

After 50+ years, I still do not trust people behind me nor do I want someone to slip up behind me and startle me. Trusting our Lord and continuing to seek His will, along with long walks, give me an inner peace of knowing He will guide me through the tough times and the good times.

My Time in Vietnam

George Howe

Sometimes I believe people go into military service with active mental problems. While serving, their problems worsen and can contribute to anxiety and obsessive-compulsive disorders. Vietnam or other combat service compounds these disorders and brings them more to the forefront for those individuals affected. These negative experiences happen so often that the individual suffers greater mental discomfort.

I went to Vietnam in 1968 with the US Navy MCB7 (Seabees) operating in Dong Ha and the DMZ. My second tour was in 1969, and I was assigned to Chu Lai. Our construction battalion built roads, hospitals, schools, wells, gun pads, and other stuff for the Marines. It was hard and dangerous work. We were routinely shot at by the enemy and shelled 1–2 times a month by artillery.

During this time, things were going on in our heads. Our lives were going by at a fast pace like there would be no tomorrow. You liked your life, but it could end anytime. You tried to forget the worry and move on. When I returned home, my Vietnam experiences made me a better person. The fear I experienced taught me to be the best I could be. Even though I thought about what happened in Vietnam, the experiences were not going to make me stop being a good person. It taught me to like life and not hurt others. If I see someone with problems, I will be there for them.

The best, I feel, that you can do is sit back, forget your problems, look at what you have done, and love people. Don't forget others or their feelings. Perhaps most of all, love your animals. They are great companions. No matter what, they will show love for you always. I sit down and talk to my animals. All my fears and concerns go away; it is a great healing and bonding time. This has been a constant activity in my healing process. I very heartily hope you try this. Animals won't judge you.

Let go of the bad stuff!

The Four Elements to My Recovery

Joe Sturdevant

On December 7, 1941, Japan bombed Pearl Harbor to ashes and mud. I was 2 ½ months old in southern California, a few miles from the Lockheed aircraft factory in Burbank where our bombers were being built. My early years were punctuated by air-raid sirens in the middle of the night, camouflage netting covering factories and businesses so they would look like farmland from the air, blackouts, and P-51s making practice strafing runs at the small airport near my house. I grew up knowing that war was no "game."

When I graduated from college, I enlisted in the army with the option to attend officer candidate school (OCS) at the Infantry School at Fort Benning, Georgia. I was commissioned in '65, got married, welcomed a baby, was sent to flight school, and got on a ship to Vietnam in October '67.

My in country orientation was flying CH-47 (Chinooks) for insertions, extractions, and resupply at the battle of Dak To in November. In January '68, I was transferred to I Corps just in time for Tet, and the action was nonstop.

On May 12, as I was leading a formation of four Chinooks in the approach to a landing zone (LZ) to extract a rifle company, my aircraft was hit by automatic weapons fire on both sides. Tracers came through the fuel tanks, and burning fuel came into the cargo bay. I made a barely controlled descent to a makeshift runway in a Special Forces camp named Kham Duc that had been surrounded by the 2d NVA Div (North

Vietnamese Army Division). Although the aircraft "tumbled" after reaching the ground, all my crew made it out. Following about five hours of ground action, we were lifted out safely by medevac. One hour later, a C-130 attempting to evacuate over 360 US civilians and Civilian Irregular Defense Group (CIDG) members was shot down in the same area where my aircraft had been hit, but all were lost. Throughout the day, morning and afternoon, casualties mounted. There's a troubling question I've always held: Why did I make it and they didn't?

I made it home at the end of '68 to a time of rage and public hostility toward the military that isolated all veterans. I was stationed at Fort Benning where soldiers were not allowed out of our cars off base if we were in uniform. But my wife and I settled in and welcomed another baby. At the end of the period of my obligation, I decided that, for my family's peace and safety, I needed to take the first opportunity to separate from active duty, and I did.

Back then, we never heard about PTSD, and even after I did hear about it, I thought it applied to guys who had a much worse time than I'd had in Vietnam and couldn't get through a normal day. But I did certainly have problems with anger, depression, isolation, and nightmares. I had a lot of resentment, mostly at the way Vietnam vets were treated by American civilians. Over time, my marriage unraveled and cratered, but I didn't lose my kids, and I worked hard and continued to meet all my obligations.

However, right after I got out of the military in May 1970, the first of four things happened that helped me deal with my depression and anxiety. I went to work for Ross Perot, a former naval officer who was building a high-tech company by hiring high energy, competitive, and ambitious company grade officers leaving the service, so I was surrounded by "friendlies." I had accidently managed to associate myself with people who had new and important goals, who worked hard and long to reach their goals, and who literally didn't have time to dwell on the war or what the civilians and the media were saying about it and us.

The second action I took was sustained physical exercise. For about eight years after I left Vietnam, I smoked heavily, drank too much, and gained a lot of weight. Seeing myself in a family Christmas photo was a shock, so I began a serious daily program of long, slow distance running, and I quit smoking. The physical benefits were great, but I was surprised at the positive emotional benefits. My anxiety began to diminish. My confidence increased. My fear of being in groups of people I didn't know—such as the crowd at a high school football game—disappeared. And my business performance accelerated rapidly.

The third and most important element was a new relationship with Mary, my wife of now more than 30 years. We had known each other in business for about seven years and had worked together on several projects. We discovered that we had a lot in common, including the fact that we both had a strong spiritual side. We attended some services together. After church and lunch one Sunday in Washington, D.C., she went with me for my first visit to the Vietnam War Memorial. It was a very emotional experience for me, but she was strongly supportive. Looking back, I believe my real healing began that day. We found a small church in Cypress, Texas where we made good friends, some of whom had been and continued to be burdened with difficult health and other challenges but with a courageous and abiding faith I had never witnessed before. Through them, I learned to trust a loving and forgiving God.

The fourth element was medication. During a routine physical in the early '90s, my doctor noticed symptoms of what he called "adjustment syndrome" and prescribed a mild antidepressant medicine. I took it for several years, and it helped me maintain perspective and a reasonably positive attitude even in very stressful circumstances. With his "advice and consent," I withdrew from the medication more than 15 years ago.

In summary, I believe that, in my case, the combination of all four elements—associating myself with people who are positive, motivated, and forward-looking; beginning and sustaining medium level physical activity; finding positive emotional and spiritual support; and medication—was essential to my recovery and now is a powerful motivator to me to support others who suffer similar challenges.

For Families and Loved Ones of Those Suffering with Post-Traumatic Stress Disorder (PTS)

Relationships

Trauma survivors with PTSD may have trouble with their close family relationships or friendships. The symptoms of PTSD can cause problems with trust, closeness, communication, and problem-solving. These problems may affect the way the survivor acts with others. In turn, the way a loved one responds to him or her affects the trauma survivor. A circular pattern can develop that may sometimes harm relationships.

How might trauma survivors react?

In the first weeks and months following a trauma, survivors may feel angry, detached, tense, or worried in their relationships. In time, most are able to resume their prior level of closeness in relationships. Yet 5 percent to 10 percent of survivors who develop PTSD may have lasting relationship problems.

Survivors with PTSD may feel distant from others and feel numb. They may have less interest in social or sexual activities. Because survivors feel irritable, on guard, jumpy, worried, or nervous, they may not be able to relax or be intimate. They may also feel an increased need to protect their loved ones. They may come across as tense or demanding.

The trauma survivor may often have trauma memories or flashbacks. He or she might go to great lengths to avoid such memories. Survivors may avoid any activity that could trigger a memory. If the survivor has trouble sleeping or has nightmares, both the survivor and partner may not be able to get enough rest. This may make sleeping together harder.

Survivors often struggle with intense anger and impulses. In order to suppress angry feelings and actions, they may avoid closeness. They may push away or find fault with loved ones and friends. Also drinking and drug problems, which can be an attempt to cope with PTSD, can destroy intimacy and friendships. Verbal or physical violence can occur.

In other cases, survivors may depend too much on their partners, family members, and friends. This could also include support persons such as health care providers or therapists.

Dealing with these symptoms can take up a lot of the survivor's attention. He or she may not be able to focus on the partner. It may be hard to listen carefully and make decisions together with someone else. Partners may come to feel that talking together and working as a team are not possible.

How might loved ones react?

Partners, friends, or family members may feel hurt, cutoff, or down because the survivor has not been able to get over the trauma. Loved ones may become angry or distant toward the survivor. They may feel pressured, tense, and controlled. The survivor's symptoms can make a loved one feel like he or she is living in a war zone or in constant threat of danger. Living with someone who has PTSD can sometimes lead the partner to have some of the same feelings of having been through trauma.

In some, a person who goes through a trauma may have certain common reactions. These reactions affect the people around the survivor. Family, friends, and others then react to how the survivor is behaving. This, in turn, comes back to affect the person who went through the trauma.

Trauma Types and Relationships

Certain types of "man-made" traumas can have a more severe effect on relationships. These traumas include:

- childhood sexual and physical abuse,
- rape,
- domestic violence,
- combat,
- terrorism,
- genocide,
- torture,
- kidnapping, or
- prisoner of war.

Survivors of man-made traumas often feel a lasting sense of terror, horror, endangerment, and betrayal. These feelings affect how they relate to others. They may feel like they are letting down their guard if they get close to someone else and trust them. This is not to say a survivor never feels a strong bond of love or friendship. However, a close relationship can also feel scary or dangerous to a trauma survivor.

Do all trauma survivors have relationship problems?

Many trauma survivors do not develop PTSD. Also, many people with PTSD do not have relationship problems. People with PTSD can create and maintain good relationships by:

- building a personal support network to help cope with PTSD while working on family and friend relationships,
- sharing feelings honestly and openly with respect and compassion,
- building skills at problem-solving and connecting with others, or
- including ways to play, be creative, relax, and enjoy others.

What Can Be Done to Help Someone Who Has PTSD?

Relations with others are very important for trauma survivors. Social support is one of the best things to protect against getting PTSD. Relationships can offset feelings of being alone. Relationships may also help the survivor's self-esteem. This may help reduce depression and guilt. A relationship can also give the survivor a way to help someone else. Helping others can reduce feelings of failure or feeling cutoff from others. Lastly, relationships are a source of support when coping with stress.

If you need to seek professional help, try to find a therapist who has skills in treating PTSD as well as working with couples or families. For information, please see our Resources page at the end of the book.

Many treatment approaches may be helpful for dealing with relationship issues. Options include:

- one-to-one and group therapy
- anger and stress management
- assertiveness training
- couples counseling

- family education classes
- family therapy

Source: PTSD: National Center for PTSD. www.ptsd.va.gov

> **A PERFECT RELATIONSHIP IS JUST TWO IMPERFECT PEOPLE WHO REFUSE TO GIVE UP ON EACH OTHER.**

> Instead of saying "I'm damaged, I'm broken, I have trust issues" say "I'm healing, I'm rediscovering myself, I'm starting over". Positive self talk.
>
> – Horacio Jones

Duc Lap, Vietnam 1968

Jon C. Bartine

Background

In the later part of August 1968, the NVA put a big push into the area south of Pleiku, RVN. It was a tough battle for the army. I was flight lead on at least two missions there, and on one of them, the FAC asked for our ordnance to be placed next to the most inner wire or barrier. I made the FAC confirm with the army commander to try and determine if we had people in that area. His comment was "Yes, they are best chance dead, but if you don't put it there, the rest of us will die." I still wonder to this day if I spread napalm and 20mm all over some of our own people. I did what I had to do, but it still haunts me to this day usually about 02:30 to 03:00 in the morning. Killing the enemy is one thing. Killing your own is altogether different.

My Narrative on Duc Lap

Here in Tuy Hoa, Vietnam, lots of us were sitting alert because the NVA were all over the Ban Me Thuot and the Duc Lap area. Those two areas are located near the border of Cambodia and to the south of Pleiku. For about 7 or 8 days, lots of attacks were run by the NVA on local towns and Vietnam Army outpost in that area. We had many army troops in the area, and as usual, the ARVN had their forces and families living there. Our wing and several other air bases were supporting them with scheduled and alert flight. I flew an alert mission over there at least two, if not three times, and a couple of them were under adverse weather conditions.

The army commanders were using lots of artillery and helicopter missions to help suppress these attacks, and they would intersperse our missions in between theirs when they needed some really heavy armament.

Flying in that area, we would pull off on downwind and look over into Cambodia and see the massive level of men and equipment that the Vietcong had located in that safe area, but we weren't allowed to go after them in Cambodia because of the "FU" rules of engagement that our politicians imposed on our flights. Had we been allowed to go after them in Cambodia, Laos, and the North Vietnam off-limits areas, the outcome of this conflict would have been far different. Giving a bleeding-heart politician a shot at conducting a war is and was a huge mistake. Part of our issues were that the political side of Washington, D.C. was for warning the North Vietnamese of what targets we were planning on hitting over the next week. They were usually well prepared for the upcoming missions. Looking over into Cambodia and watching them toss the finger at you was sort of a kick in the butt.

Anyway, back to the mission at hand. Army troops were in a situation of heavy contact with a well-supplied force of Vietcong. As I said before, this had been going on for several days, and I had been here a couple of other times.

The army had built a base camp in pretty much the standard way, that is, that the main camp was in the center and then they would have 3 fences that were heavily built and fortified with foxholes and berms built up for protection. Each of these looked to be about 100 to 150 feet out from the innermost fighting position. Built this way would give them a chance to fall back from the outer ones to the main camp.

On the earlier mission I had been on, they were still at the outer positions, and we were putting our ordnance outside of that area. The earlier mission, we had been approaching the target from the south with a west pull off. That was when we could see the large buildup of forces over in Cambodia. On this mission, we were working from the north to south with pull offs to the east. When on troops in contact missions, we had to be restricted to specific delivery heading because the deliveries had to be made so that long or short bombs would not go into our own personnel's position.

This mission was happening near nightfall, and the FAC was pushing to get the ordnance delivered. We got a briefing that we would be putting our napalm on the "innermost" wire. That set off alarm bells in my head as who was there and were any of our people including the ARVN troops in the trenches. I told the FAC that we would not deliver our ordnance until I had clarification from the army commander that there were no friendly troops in the area. There was a lot of delay, and it was getting darker by the minute, but finally the FAC said that the army commander was authorizing the delivery of napalm. *Not good enough*, I said in my mind. Finally the army commander came up on our frequency, I guess from a helicopter. He stated that he did not know if any US or ARVN troops were there or what their status was. In the intense fighting that had been going on, it is really easy to lose control and not know the detailed disposition of troops. He did say that if we did not deliver the napalm, everyone in the command center would be overrun and probably killed. There were about 25 to 40 troops there in the command area.

Decision time for me. I went ahead and delivered our ordnance on the inner wire area to the west of the command area.

We were receiving some ground fire initially from that area, but after 8 cans of napalm were dropped, it was really quiet.

If I remember right, the BDA (battle damage assessment) was vague about the results on enemy troops. You must see the results of a delivery of napalm to know what it does. It is a thick liquid that spreads, sticks, and burns very hot. When the can hits the ground, it is set off by a phosphorous charge that causes it to burn. It rolls into crevasses, sticks to people, and basically leaves the area charred and burnt. They say it sucks the breath out of people who are near it.

To this day, I think about the US and ARVN (South Vietnamese) troops that could have been in that area. Alive, wounded, or dead, I still wonder what we really did. And on top of that, my wingman and I put 1,600 rounds of 20mm HEI in the area to insure complete and total destruction of the area. I wonder who was there. Were they alive, wounded, dead or…?. Like I have said before, I did what I had to do. You just always hope you don't have to hurt or kill your own people.

The one big thing that all fighter pilots worried about was what is called a "short round." That is when you are dropping your weapons and screw up and don't hit the designated target but drop it on your own troops (fratricide or friendly fire). This didn't happen often but usually happened when you had a new inexperienced pilot or more likely when you have an REMF flying with you.

This whole thing has really surfaced big time since about the mid to late 1990s and especially since I started attending Warrior Group sessions at Camp Hope. I have been going there every Thursday night for dinner and meetings for three years, and just the visual look at the younger troops basically kicks this memory off. I refuse to quit going, as I have made a lot of friends and truly believe that some of us old guys are a vital asset to the younger bunch. I also will not let this thing beat me into giving up. Thinking about the alternative is not really good.

I sometimes wake up at night in bed and visualize I am there as if I am wounded on the ground and watch this F-100 coming at me. I see the napalm cans come off the wing, tumble, roll side to side and end over end, then see them hit the ground. Then in really slow, slow, slow motion, I see the cans bust open and ignite, and then the fireball slowly rolls across my body and the others around me. Then, the lights go out. I snap back into reality and I am up sitting in my airplane pulling off the target looking back at the burning place I just dropped the napalm.

About this time, Suzie, my German shepherd, is lying down beside me. How the hell does she know and understand? Sometimes I think she is what gets me through the rest of the night. To think that she showed up at my front door as a dumped stray wanting to come in my house 8 years ago as a 4-week-old pup is beyond me.

These thoughts and remembrances are usually kicked off after I wake up in the middle of the night in a cold panic after somehow realizing that I have just recovered from my screwup on the mission to Laos. One of the mentors at Camp Hope says that probably the 3 spurs in my neck start hurting and wake me up. I contend that the spurs came from the 14g recovery that I had to do in Laos earlier that year to stay out of scattering myself all over Laos.

I have to be careful during the day, as if I start thinking about these items, I start gritting me teeth and basically just come to a mental stop for the rest of the day. Usually if it gets to me big-time during the day or night, I just go get in the car and go drive and drive. No idea where I am going.

Here is the web address of what it was like for an army helicopter pilot in the same conflict: www.yankeeairpirate.com/ShotDownAtDucLap.html. We were fighter pilots and saw the war at seven hundred feet per second. These helicopter pilots were right in the thick of the battle. Enough. I can't write anymore.

Kon Tum

Jon C. Bartine

I flew 336 combat missions in Vietnam and Laos during my tour from September 17, 1967 to September 15, 1968. During that time, I estimate that I was involved in killing between 2,000 and 5,000 people. A letter from the wing commander documents the KIA at Kon Tum City at 972 people. I was on 2 of the litter flights during that conflict. In actuality, there should have been 973 KIA listed, but the one I knocked off a hill was probably never found because of the crevice that he fell into when I used the downwash of the airplane to knock him off that hill. To this day, I sometimes wonder who he was. I now strongly believe that he was a local farm boy who was just watching the air show.

I was assigned the day alert schedule on January 30, 1968 through February 2, 1968 and reported for alert duty at about 6:30 in the morning. First thing to be done is go to the squadron building to get a good detailed weather briefing for the day and then on to intelligence to get a general idea of the overall conflict situation in Vietnam. They mentioned in the briefing that the Kon Tum area was experiencing some action, but nothing was too serious yet. After the briefings and the weather briefing, we got a ride on the flight line truck to the revetments where the alert birds were located.

Before you go fly any USAF aircraft, you are required to do a detailed inspection of the aircraft systems, weapons systems, and overall condition of the aircraft. Mine checked out. On this flight, I had 800 rounds of 20mm HEI (high explosive incendiary) ammo. To describe HEI ammo is to say that I had 800 three-quarter-inch hand grenades that the guns could spit out at 6,000 rounds per minute or 100 rounds per second. Really a good weapon for troops in the open. I also had 4 Mark 82 high-drag bombs. The high-drag bomb had 4 fins that opened when released and slowed the bomb down so that we could get in close and deliver them with far more accuracy. This also slowed the bomb down so that it was 1,000 to 1,500 feet behind the airplane, allowing the airplane to be out of the bomb blast and shrapnel area.

Preflight done and the cockpit arranged for a quick departure, we went into the alert shack to settle in and await for the bell to ring. When on alert, you either read a book, took a nap, or played cards. I'm not sure what I was doing, but at about 10 a.m., the bell rang and the wing command post said to scramble Litter 01 and 02. That would be us. I was flying wing this day, so I scrambled out to the aircraft, climbed the ladder, strapped in with the crew chief's help, and pulled the ejection seat safety pins, while all the time you are pushing the start button, advancing the throttle to the start position, and monitoring the engine gauges to ensure it was starting properly. Alert birds were scheduled to be off the ground in 15 minutes, so no mistakes or goofing off. After assuring that you were strapped in properly, the crew chief would be down on the ground, removing the ladder and waiting for you to signal that the brakes were activated, and he would remove the wooden chocks that secured the aircraft while in the revetment.

Litter 1, the flight leader, calls for "Litter 1 check in and taxi," and I answered, "Litter 2." Ground control has been notified we are coming and automatically clears Litter 1 and 2 to taxi to the arming area. There was no need to look for your crew chief, as he was already out in front of the airplane, signally clear to taxi and signally for a right turn. Once out and turned, you always got the big salute and thumbs-up from the crew chief.

Once in the arming area, the procedure is to set the brakes, hands, and arms out of the cockpit and, on the side rails while the arming crew pulls the safety pins, charges the guns and ensures that the weapons are ready to be released. Once armed up, Litter 1 hand signals to change to the tower frequency and says, "Litter 1 and 2 ready for departure." I answer with just "2" to let him know I am on frequency. Canopy is down, aircraft into position at the end of the runway, and lead twirls his finger for engine run-up.

Takeoff in the F-100D model was about 7 to 8 thousand feet to takeoff roll. Preparing for takeoff was brakes on, push the throttle up (not too fast or you would get compressor stalls), and monitor the gauges for proper engine acceleration and power. Lead signaled with a head nod, indicating that he was moving, and lit his afterburner with a bang, and I start counting to 10 before I release my brakes and light the afterburner. While accelerating to lift off with a speed of 180 knots (207 mph), you look ahead for any possibility of an abort by lead, check the engines, and monitor the speed. At about 170 knots, you rotate the airplane to about 10 or 12 degrees and off the ground at 180 knots. Now it's time to clean up the airplane with gear up, and once they are in up and locked, you move the flap switch to the retracted position. Joining up with the lead aircraft became second nature after a lot of missions and you just accelerated to 350 KIAs and got inside the turnout of traffic circle as lead turned to the northwest heading toward Kon Tum. All the time you monitor the engine instruments, change to departure frequency when prompted by lead, and join up on his wing. Both of us checked each other over after joining up, looking for anything abnormal as we climbed to our cruising altitude of 22,000 ft. Climbing any higher on a flight that required 25 minutes en route was just a waste of fuel.

At this point, departure control would tell us to contact mission control, who would then assign us an FAC (forward air controller) who was in charge of the air assets that would be used on the target. Over on the FAC's frequency, Litter 1 told him that our ordnance was 4 napalm, 4,500-pound high drags, and each of us had 800 rounds of 20mm HEI. He briefed us that this was a "troops in contact" situation and a significant amount of NVA (North Vietnam Army) troops were in the area, mostly to the north and west of the base camp area. He told us that all the US Army and South Vietnamese personnel were inside the base camp. Also, he stated that the NVA were approaching the outer wire. US Army and Marine Corps base camps normally consisted of the base camp in the center and then 3 rings of concertina wire and abutments going out about 500 ft. The FAC wanted me to put the 500 lbs. of high drags about 500 ft. to the north of the base camp outer concertina wire and lead to use his napalm just outside of the outer concertina wire. The FAC said he was into mark with a 2.75 Willy Peter (white phosphorus) rocket which would put out a lot of white smoke when it hit the ground. These FACs were very good at marking the target, and he said for lead to put his napalm on his mark from an east-to-west run-in. He told me to put my bomb north of that 500 ft. area.

Lead was in and delivered his right on target. As I was rolling in, I could see ground fire at lead from the area that I was assigned to hit. I informed him he was taking fire, and I watched him roll right then rapidly back to the left to throw the gunners off. As I came down the slide to release my bombs, I could not see any NVA or ground fire, and I put my two outer 500 lb. bombs into the target area. The weapons system on the F-100 wouldn't let you drop the outside bomb separately. Asymmetrical wing loads would accrue if you did that and would cause a rolling moment toward the remaining bomb. There was a way to play with the circuit breakers to fool the systems, but we didn't do that on this flight. On the pull off, we had to pull up into a steep hill that had a vertical cliff on the back side. As I was pulling off, I noticed this one guy standing on the top edge of this cliff. This cliff was about 1/2 mile west of the target area.

The FAC said, "Hold high and dry for a minute" while he assessed the damage. He then came back on and told lead to release one napalm short of his last one and the other napalm long. Basically same heading, same procedures. The issue with coming in from the same direction and altitude is that it is one hell of a good way to get a few holes punched in your aircraft. So far, we had been lucky. This was pretty much the same procedure used on all missions that had troops in contact. Dropping bomb or napalm or shooting the guns directed toward the troops was a no-no. I only know of one time that was done, and that was because the troops were caught in a valley with steep hills on either side, which dictated the direction of delivery. Lead called in and dropped his napalm right on target but was still taking some fire from the north. The FAC told me to put my next bombs just a little closer to the base camp but one short of my last ones and one long. After doing that and then on the pull off, knowing we were being shot at, I employed the procedure my check pilot taught me on my first and second mission as a newbie. Warren Standard, my check out instructor pilot would sit in the back seat of the 2-seat F-100, and on pull off he would yell, "Jink, goddamn it!" Those are three words I will never forget. I still hear those command word, and to this day, I hear them sometimes at night. What he wanted was for me to put 5 gs on the aircraft once the nose of the aircraft was 20 to 30 degrees above the horizon to roll hard right in this case and then roll hard left. That means that I would roll hard right 20 degrees of heading and then back the other direction about 120 degrees to get up on the cross leg.

The NVA usually had one guy who was good shot and a bunch of others who merely pointed their guns in the direction of his gun. That made for lots of bullets from their auto AK-47 concentrated in your direction. I am convinced that this jink procedure that Warren Standard taught me kept me from ever being hit. I flew 336 combat missions and never took a bullet. By using this procedure, you caused total confusion in the guys who were just shooting in the direction of the lead aimer. I was the only guy in the entire wing of 125 pilots who managed to skate without a hit. I was scheduled to fly 340 missions, but on 336, I said "Fu——it" and landed and went to the bar. The ops officer said they had been expecting my stand-down from flying for a couple of days. I had reached the point where I knew I was going to be the guy who got the "magic" bullet on the next flight.

The FAC wanted us to hold high and dry again. He was assessing the target area. He re-marked the target and wanted us to put our 20 mm in the same area. On the first pass, lead and I laid 20 mm rounds all over the area that we had been bombing. Usually we would shoot for 3 to 4 seconds, which would take about half of the rounds. On the first pass, I noticed my guy on the hill still standing there. He was right up on the very top next to the big drop-off. Next pass was the same, basically covering the entire area to the north of the target with our little 20 mm HEI hand grenades. On this pass, I watched my little man on the pull off, and he just stood there in the squatting position watching the air show. I made up my mind that on the next one, life would get a lot harder.

The third gun pass was much the same. Most of the ground fire had stopped, so I went after the guy standing on the hill.

As I pulled off, not worrying about ground fire, I went up the steep incline at about a 100 feet, and as I approached him, he stood up from his squatting position. I was still about 75 to 100 feet off the trees, then I pulled 4 or 5 gs on the airplane. Doing this maneuver pushed a lot of downwash from the wings and basically knocked him backward off the hill. As I pulled off the target (man on the hill), I rolled hard left and nearly upside down, and I watched him go over the side and fall, I would estimate, 300 to 500 feet down into the crevice. I guess his body is still there today.

The FAC said to hold high and dry, and he would get BDA (bomb damage assessment) and KIA (killed in action) to us later. We checked out with him and departed back for Tuy Hoa. Back at base, the landing was uneventful, and neither of us had any aircraft issues, so we went back to the revetment for fuel, bombs, napalm, and 20mm ammo.

On alert status a day later, settling in for another good nap after the aircraft was preflighted, the good old alert bell rang about 3 p.m. and ordered, "Launch litter 1 and 2." Same drill getting in, started, checked out and off the ground. Once we were in the Kon Tum area, we had a different FAC. He was still concentrating on the same areas as before. After we had delivered our bombs and napalm, we were asking to once more shoot the guns. By the way, dropping bombs was okay, but the plum job was shooting the guns. Damn, we loved to shoot the guns. I made two passes shooting, and when I pulled up on the downwind, I did an instrument check. When you were on downwind, you always looked the aircraft and instrument over. My eyes scanned the gauges and *yikes, gasp, zero oil pressure.* Son of a bitch!

That is just about the kiss of death for the J57 engine in the F-100. The rule of thumb was that when the oil pressure went to zero and then the oil temperature light came on, you had about 1 minute before the engine would seize. You needed to either get the aircraft on the ground or get to check out the ejection system. I informed lead that I had a problem and turned southeast for Pleiku AB about 30 miles away. In about 30 seconds, litter 01 was on my wing and told me that I wasn't leaking oil or burning and that it didn't show any bullet holes that he could see.

Pleiku was an outlying base that had a 6000-foot long runway. It was one of our emergency landing sites and had been equipped with a barrier-arresting system to stop the aircraft. How that worked was that a big, stout cable was across the runway about 1000 feet from the far end of the runway. It had a big brake on each side of the runway that would take up the cable and increase the pressure as the cable was played out behind the airplane when the tailhook engaged it. Very similar to a navy carrier landing but not as violent.

The other issue when landing with zero oil pressure was that the F-100 did not have a zero or zero ejection system. The zero or zero ejection system was developed later for the F-4 and other aircraft. The ejection system was built so that you could be sitting still on the ramp, not moving, and eject from the aircraft. Most of the time, the chute opened before your feet touched the ground. It was propelled by an initial charge that would start the seat up the rails and then had a set of rockets that lit up and put you 400 to 500 feet in the air. Magic seat actuation also started and unlatched the seat belts, a butt strap slammed tight, and threw you out of the seat all the while actuating the chute deployment. All the pilot had to do was hang on, pray, and try to land feetfirst.

To successfully get out of the F-100 airplane, you need to have 180 knots forward speed at the time you started the ejection process and a positive 500-feet-per-minute climb rate. Once you started the ejection sequence, you were blasted out of the aircraft with hard lighting explosive charges. Then you'd hope you didn't get a back compression. You had to push away from the seat after opening the seat belt and hope you had hooked up the "D ring." The D ring was attached to the seat and, if hooked up, pulled the chute lanyard, thus pulling the drogue chute which, in turn, pull the main chute. Lots of hoping and praying here. Anything less than that speed and upward velocity and the pilot could not separate from the seat, deploy the parachute, and have it open before the ground reached up and bashed you. If I remember right, not having those parameters was referred to as another "coffin corner."

The other issue was that the F-100 took 7,000 ft. to stop on a normal runway. That is why we had 10,000 feet at Tuy Hoa plus 1,000-foot overruns at each end. Pleiku only had 6,000 ft. plus 400 or 500-ft. overruns. The other issue coming into play was that in order to get the 180 KIAs or 500-feet-per-minute parameter you needed to fly final approach at 210 IAS when normal final speed was 165 plus fuel. This extra speed allowed you to rotate the airplane from the landing angle of about 3 to 5 degrees down to a 10 to 15-degree climb angle and still have the 150 KIAs and 500 feet per minute for ejection. Flying final at the 210 basically throws the 7,000-foot normal landing distance out the window. Anyway, I flew final at 210 KIAs and touched down at the beginning of the short overrun.

Luckily the F-100 had a parachute and locked wheel antiskid. The brakes could be fully applied before touchdown, and you would not blow the tires. I put the chute out just before touchdown and had the brakes fully applied. On the runway, with full anti-skid working, there is a lot of cycling of the brakes. I felt the chute hit and watched as the other end of the runway was coming toward me. Lying down on the brakes this hard was always a big chance of blowing one or both tires.

Another thing about Pleiku was that at the end of that runway was a big drop-off into the dump. Luckily the brakes did their job, the tires stayed up, and the 'chute worked, and as I approached the safety barrier, I retracted the speed brake and let the tailhook down. All in all, after engaging the barrier, I ended up stopping about 300 feet from the end of the runway. I could see over the end into the dump. Believe me that was not an inviting place. Now, the amazing thing was the engine was sitting there at idle. Zero oil pressure but running fine. WTF?

Looking back, maintenance found a broken wire to the oil pressure gauge, two worn-out brakes and two main tires that were at the bottom of the wear cords. I spent a night in the officers' club bar, having a drink or two or three or…or…or. I got a ride back to Tuy Hoa on the Gooney Bird shuttle the next day, but before I left, the fire chief took me out to the runway. He wanted to show me something. Starting in the overrun where I touched down all the way to the barrier were two black marks from the tires.

The final analysis of this 3–4-day mission was 972 enemies were killed in action, and it was by actual body count. Those of us who participated in the troops in contact mission at Kon Tum got a letter from the air force liaison officer which resulted in one of the two Distinguished Flying Crosses that I got in Vietnam. (I still think that letter with 972 KIA should be corrected to 973 KIA.) Just another day in Vietnam!

Why do I write about the little man on the hill? Well, here we are years later, and I have had bad dreams about many of the things that happened while flying there in Vietnam. Today I wonder and think about who he was, what he was doing there, why he was there, and really who he was? My thoughts have gone from enemy command soldier to "Joe Schmuck" watching the air show. Never once did I see him act like he was pointing a gun or directing anything of that nature, or maybe he was the

NVA commander directing the fight. You must remember he was at least a 1/2 mile or more from the battle area. Another one of the nightmares. There are about 8 to 10 of those that wake me up.

The Saga of Bent Bent Four

Jon C. Bartine

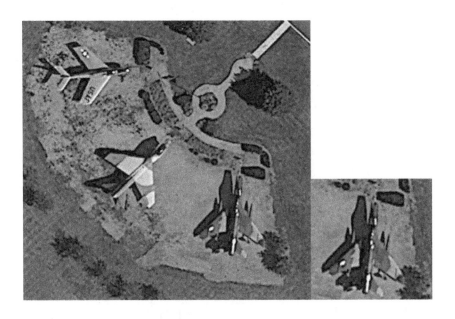

Sometime in July or August 1968, my friend and I were sitting night alert. At about 1 a.m., we were rousted out of bed and told we were we being scrambled for a flight into the southern part of Laos. Out to the airplane, start, taxi, arm, and take off. Once off the ground and joined up, we climb to about 25,000 feet because we had farther to go than the usual alert mission. Not exactly sure of where the target was in Laos, but it was in the Salavan, Laos's area. That makes it 30 to 40 minutes flying time, which would stretch our fuel. The normal procedures of control were used, and we were told that we would meet the FAC and that a C-130 would be here to illuminate the target. We were also told that it was a 37mm gun site that was actively shooting. There must have been some "not supposed to be United States people there" in Laos. Anyway, briefed by the FAC (forward air controller) and waiting for the C-130 (a large 4-engine turbo prop that was used for troop and cargo movement) to arrive, we continued to burn fuel. After a few minutes, the FAC informed us that the C-130 had had engine problems and wouldn't be there for the mission. Smart aircraft commander.

The country of Laos was basically off-limits in the Vietnam conflict, but in reality, it was as involved in the Vietnam conflict as much as North and South Vietnam. The one thing that was different about Laos was that it was controlled by several tribal factions and they were big in the drug trade. The never discussed CIA was there. They were using their DC-3s (a smaller two-engine cargo aircraft), short field aircraft, and helicopters to manage this "off-limits country." Well, we were there. I have one piece of paper stating that I have 17 missions in Laos. I guess I just flew over on training missions. LOL.

Anyway, it was a clear night but dark, dark, dark. The FAC wanted to continue and said he had small flares that he could throw out the side window. The flare that the C-130 was going to drop was about 3–4 feet long and 10–12 inches around. Three of those would make the target world light up like daylight. The FAC's flares were about 12–18 inches long and 2–3 inches round, kind of like lighting a small candle in a football stadium at night. When he threw a couple of them out the window, it effectively lit his aircraft up, and the 37mm started shooting at him. By doing that, the gun site also showed us its location, but keeping track of it without defined references which we would have had if we were working under the C-130 flares was next to impossible.

The FAC said he was going to put a Willie Peter (White Phosphorus) marking rocket in the target area. He also said it was all bad guy country, so rolling into the target from any direction was at our discretion. His statement of it was all "bad guy country," and it meant that there were no friendlies in the area and that we didn't need to concern ourselves with the normal rules of engagement. He threw out a couple of more flares and marked the target then pulled up and tossed out a couple of more flares. With his little flares, we could see the mark, and as always, he said, "Hit my mark."

I was flying 2, and my buddy was leading. He said he was rolling in from the north and dropped his bombs slightly to the left of mark. Watching this indicated to me that the wind that would affect the aircraft and bomb was out of the west. As he was delivering his ordnance, I continued so that I could come around and roll in from the west. As he was pulling off the target, the 37mm opened up on him. When the 37mm quit shooting at him, he started blindly shooting out in my direction. I think the 37mm shooter knew from past experience that the next airplane would probably come from the west. Planning on aiming a little bit short of the mark, I rolled in from the west and started down the slide.

The FAC said earlier that the target elevation was about 1,500 (that's a WAG or "wild ass guess") feet, so using a 45-degree dive angle and 450 IAS, I would drop at 4,500 feet plus the 1,500 elevation of the target. My altimeter would read 6,000 feet when I released my bombs. Looking back on this incident, I think one of the reasons that I got into this mess was that I didn't take the tailwind factor into my roll in. How this would affect you at nighttime was that as you did the roll in from heading south to an easterly drop heading. What the wind would do all the while time you were flying was displace you east as the wind was almost always out of the west. During the daytime, you would pick this up and compensate for it. However, at night, you lose your air-to-ground references, and picking up this displacement would not be possible. What this did was put me closer to the target than I had planned and cause me to roll into the target at a steeper angle. You also need to remember that I had tracers all over the area I was in. The big problem with tracers is that you only get to see every 4th or 5th bullet. They normally loaded the guns with tracers every 4th or 5th round, using the tracer to light up path as a director to lead and track an aircraft.

Well, now all hell breaks loose. I am not sure how I got as steep as I did, but when I looked down at the altitude indicator, I was reading 58 degrees. That number is planted deep in the memory, and I can still, to this day, see the altitude indicator display. I wake up at night sometimes, and that instrument is the first thing I see. Bad words were all I could think. The indicated airspeed was passing 500 IAS (indicated airspeed). Another double holy crap. Now the altitude instrument comes in to play. Damn! Damn! Damn! It was passing downward through about 5,500 feet. 500 feet too low for a 45-degree angle but 2,000 feet too low for a 60-degree dive angle. A 60-degree dive angle delivery was seldom used and would have required releasing the bombs at 6,000 ft. plus the 1,500 target elevation and 7,500 ft. on the altitude indicator. I was well below that number.

The reason for dropping your bombs at 4,500 feet AGL (above ground level) for 45-degree dive angle and 6,000 feet for 60-degree dive angle was that these altitudes provided you with a recovery altitude of 1,800 to 2,000 ft. above the ground. This safety factor kept you out of the bomb blast area and provided some protection from small arms fire.

I'm in big trouble! You must remember that all of this happens at "warp speed." 500 knots is almost 850 feet per second. Cross-checks on instruments, flight control inputs, and thoughts go on a warp speed. In that microsecond of thought, a million things went through my mind. Dump all the bombs was the first one. Three pushes on the release pickle button on the stick and thoughts of how to recover from this mess went through my mind as well.

Now it seems like time stopped there in midair. My mind went back to the bar at Luke AFB, Arizona about a year before in upgrade training. After flying, we would go to the stag bar at the officers' club there and bullshit, brag, and learn. One of the instructors one night gave me my out. He said if you ever get "*too steep, too fast, and too low,* here is your procedure. Engine idle, speed brakes out, pull the control stick all the way aft against the seat, and pray." Those were his exact words. He said the "G Load" will be big. As I said, all of this happened in my mind in a nanosecond. I followed the procedures to the letter, and the nose of the aircraft seemed like it took forever to start to come up. I felt the G Load begin and watched the attitude indicator begin to move slowly toward the level position. I was fighting hard to stay conscious, as I knew if I let the blood drain from my head, I would pass out and then "buy the farm," as they say. That is about when I lost control of my neck muscles because of the G loading. I really strained hard to keep my head upright. It seemed as if the slab (aft control surface) got hold of the airflow, and the airplane nose started to slowly start coming up. I can remember my head beginning to be pulled down and then suddenly being plastered on my chest as I lost control of my neck and back muscles. All I could see and focus on was the attitude indicator looking through the tops of my eyes. Slow but sure, it started coming toward the level position as my body shrank further down in the seat. My thoughts were *Maybe I will make it*. If you hit the ground at this speed, it is quick, and little is left but little, tiny chunks of your body, and the airplane would be scattered for over a half mile, never to be recovered.

Several years later, when I was stationed in Spain flying the F-100 and I was at the gunnery range in north Spain as an observer, on the gunnery range, the pilots would drop practice bombs and shoot their 20mm guns. There were definite rules and procedures as far as altitudes and speeds were concerned. We had a flight of 4 working and a couple of the pilots were REMF (a deskman in headquarters referred to as a Rear Echelon Motherf——er). These guys didn't get what the game of being a fighter pilot was but were great at the desk and usually were just flying to meet the monthly flying requirement. Lead 3 and 4 were doing okay, but number 2 seemed to be a little spooky on the radio transmissions and flight actions. Sitting in the tower just off to the side, you could watch everything they were doing when delivering their weapons. When they got down to shooting the guns, 2 was having some issue lining up on his first pass, but nothing we thought was too dangerous. On his second last pass, he stopped shooting late, and the range controller had already called a "foul" on him. He was inside the 1,500-foot stop shooting line. On the next pass, the range office called another foul on him, but he didn't begin to recover from the 10-degree dive angle. Apparently when the controller called foul, he was jolted from "target fixation" and started to make his recovery, but it was too late and not aggressive enough. At the last second, he jerked the nose of the aircraft up 20 degrees. The aircraft hit the ground just about level and created a huge dust cloud. It then came up off the ground about 20 feet and disintegrated into a million pieces. I am thinking that's me if I had hit the ground in Laos.

We of course stared at it for a few seconds, not believing our eyes, then called the home base command post to deliver the sad news. About an hour later, the base chopper showed up with the investigation team. The flight surgeon was the leadman.

He looked the situation over and said—believe it or not—"Let's go to town and have lunch." Huhuhu! I'll never forget that statement. We all looked at one another and got in the car and went to town with him and had lunch. Couple of hours later, we returned to the wreck site and the flight surgeon's instructions were "Look for the flies." More words to never forget. The biggest pieces we found were his feet still in his flight boots. My thoughts were *But for the grace and help of God there I am in Laos.*

Sometimes luck and the upper being will save you. Many times when I wake up at night and have a nightmare of this incident, I first feel my head slam down on my chest then see the trees flash by the canopy and then see this aircraft hit the ground and disintegrate into a million pieces with me in the middle of the debris.

Back to my big screwup, my only real thoughts and comments were "God save me and I will be a good boy forever." The next thing I realize and see at the same time is a climb attitude on the attitude indicator, and out of my peripheral vision, I realized that I saw the trees go by on each side. I still, to this day, think I bottomed out in a river or a small valley because I distinctly remember the tree right beside both sides of the canopy. *Wow* I am still alive! *Wow!* I look at the G meter, and it is pegged at 10 gs, its maximum reading.

I am not sure what I thought at the time, but when I relive this major event in my life, I still wonder what I thought, how I thought, and why I thought. I will wake up at night, eyes wide open and with a heart rate out of control. I really should have been scattered all over Laos. Just my feet still in my boots.

The other thing that still amazes me was that the aircraft did not get any damage from the blast and shrapnel of the bombs. These bombs were two 1,000 pounders and two 750-pound slicks. They must have gone off fairly close to the aircraft flight path, or maybe they were released too low to run the fuse timers out.

Pulling up on downwind, I informed lead that I have dropped all my bombs on that pass and would be holding "high and dry." That means that I would not be making another pass. Looking at my G meter again, it really showed pegged at 10 gs. Didn't surprise me. The slab on the F-100, that is, the horizontal control surface on the back, would go down almost 45 degrees. At those speeds, that is one hell of a control moment.

Lead made another pass and dropped his last two bombs and called for join up. My comment was "FU." Those were the exact words I said. I wasn't getting close to anyone for a while. He told me later that the tone of my voice told him that something serious had happened that I wasn't talking about. I followed him back to Tuy Hoa, our home base, at about 1,500 feet in trail off to the side. I had some concern about the operation of the gear and flaps, but they all worked as designed.

Landing was uneventful, but now I must face the crew chief and maintenance. I knew that the aircraft would have to go in for at least an "over G" inspection. I called the line chief to meet us because I was sure there would be some damage to the aircraft. Normal G loading on pull off was 4 to 5 gs, and max would be 7. We looked the airplane over and found rivets and fasteners on the bottom of the airplane between the wing, and the fuselage popped. But the most stunning thing to me was the outer tips of the horizontal slap were bent down at about 30 to 45 degrees. This poor airplane had just had the hell "G'd" out of it. The line chief redlined it, and we knew it would be out of commission for a while. In the end, I think I bought the crew chief and others working to repair the airplane about 6 cases of beer. I met my friend at the alert shack, and he asked me what happened. I gave him a short brief and another FU, and we left for the hutch area.

That night, I sat in the hooch and looked at an unopened bottle of Jim Beam and said it was the only way. I had to get rid of the effects of adrenaline and stress. My body was wound tight from that adventure, and sleep was going to be sometime the next day. All in all, that bottle didn't affect me. I sat there in the hooch, stared at the wall, relived the pull off—the trees flashing by over and over—and drank the whole damn bottle. It really seemed to have no effect, and it was just being used to kill the effects of the adrenaline that had been pumped into my body.

The next day, my back muscles and neck hurt to the unbearable level. I went to the flight surgeon, and he gave me some magic stuff and said, "Give it a day or so." In retrospect, in 1994, I got tired of my neck still hurting, and I had an MRI. The results were 3 spurs in 4, 5, and 6. They still bother me at night and bring this whole episode back to light. I wake up feeling my head slam down on my chest and see the trees flash by.

Making light of the situation, the F-100 involved in this was number 884. I renamed it "Bent Bent Four." A couple of days later, when I was delivering another case of beer to the crew chief, he informed me that this airplane was a "lead the fleet aircraft" and had a magic box in the wheel well that had logged 14 gs, the maximum it would record for over 5 seconds. Didn't surprise me at all. My 175 lbs. weight during the pull of 14 plus gs was about 2,500 plus lbs. Kind of sinks your butt in the seat of the airplane. Now that I just wrote this, I feel as if I am about to explode. Just another mission in Vietnam. LOL!

On a sad note to this event, I couldn't remember the instructor pilot who told us this info on the recovery procedure in the bar. It was "straight arrow." I couldn't remember his name, and finally one of the guys in the Super Sabre Society e-mailed me that it was Paul Philips. I got this info in March of 2017 and had a trip coming up to the factory in Thailand, so I put it on my list to find him when I got back and call him and relate how valuable his teaching was to me and my life. I got home the end of May, and the first of June, I got the word that Paul Philips had passed away. I really wanted to tell him how his time and instruction info was of value to me. Still bothers me that I was unable to just say thank you.

The other crazy part of this is that a friend of mine told me this aircraft was located at Rickenbacker ANG base in Columbus, Ohio. Just goes to show that some of us old dogs are hard to get rid of. In the fall of 2017, I scheduled a trip to Columbus, Ohio, and did a photo shoot with the PIO officer there. Doing this photo shoot (see attached photos) with David Webb and Roger Dimick is one of the highlights of my old age. Being around and looking, touching, and thinking about the aircraft that saved your butt 50 years ago was a real emotional experience. *Fantastic!* Thank you!

Now how do I deal with this situation? I wake up at night with the spurs in my neck hurting, dreaming and thinking about the "G load" and trees flashing by. I usually just lie there, pet my dog, and thank God that I am still alive. Going to Camp Hope for PTSD sessions has helped to deal with this, and writing this article for the peer group book has been really good. When I reread this article, I live it all over again and again, but it has helped make me realize how lucky I am to be here to write this.

Thank you for reading this.

HELP Is on the Way! "STRESSORS"

W.S. "Stan" Wright

History Will Repeat!

Sometimes things happen to people that are unusually or especially frightening, horrible, or traumatic. Consider these examples: a serious accident or fire, physical abuse, sexual assault, earthquakes, floods, war or seeing someone be killed or seriously injured or having a loved one die through homicide or suicide. These are stressors that must be confronted.

There is information that suggests a correlation between the physical activities experienced and the gradual age-old issue of age—the physical and emotional degeneration that we all experience. Some of these symptoms can be treated with medications, physical activity, and physical treatment.

Have you ever experienced a serious accident or fire, physical abuse, sexual assault, an earthquake, a flood, war, or seeing someone killed or seriously injured or having a loved one die through homicide or suicide? People with PTSD often try to avoid things that remind them of the trauma. This can help you feel better in the moment, but in the long term, it can keep you from recovering from PTSD.

In therapy, conditions known as motor systems disorders affecting neurological disorders will expose you to the thoughts, feelings, and situations that you've been avoiding to "confront." It sounds scary, but facing things you're afraid of in a safe way can help you learn that you don't need to avoid reminders of the trauma. Daily stressors have increased suicide rates among veterans of our current military conflicts at a greater rate in comparison to the general public.

Emotional Balance and Education

PTSD symptoms include disturbing thoughts, feelings, or dreams related to the events; mental or physical distress to trauma-related cues; attempts to avoid trauma-related cues; alterations in how a person thinks and feels; and an increase in the fight-or-flight response. These symptoms last for more than a month after the event.

Symptoms of PTSD generally begin within the first 3 months after the inciting traumatic event but may not begin until years later. In the typical case, the individual with PTSD persistently avoids trauma-related thoughts and emotions and discussion of the traumatic event and may even have amnesia of the event. However, the event is commonly relived by the individual through intrusive, recurrent recollections, dissociative episodes of reliving the trauma ("flashbacks"), and nightmares.

While it is common to have symptoms after any traumatic event, the symptoms must persist to a sufficient degree (i.e., causing dysfunction in life or clinical levels of distress) for longer than one month after the trauma to be classified as PTSD. According to the VA and others, there are four types of PTSD symptoms, but they may not be the same for everyone. Each person experiences symptoms in their own way. Flashbacks, nightmares, or memories of the trauma can happen because of a stressor. For example, seeing a news report about a disaster may trigger someone who lived through a hurricane, or hearing a car backfire might bring back memories of gunfire for a combat veteran. Things that remind you of a particular event or stressor can cause you to avoid certain people or situations that remind you of the event. Someone who was assaulted on the bus might avoid taking public transportation. A combat veteran may avoid crowded places like shopping malls because it feels dangerous to be around so many people. You may also try to stay busy all the time so you don't have to talk or think about the event.

You may be sad or numb and lose interest in things that were once enjoyable, like spending time with friends. You may feel that the world is dangerous and that you can't trust anyone. It may be hard for you to feel or express happiness or other positive feelings. It's common to feel jittery or "keyed up" like it's hard to relax. This is called *hyperarousal*. You might have trouble sleeping and concentrating or you may feel like you're always on the lookout for danger. You may suddenly get angry and irritable, and if someone surprises you, you might startle easily.

Life Events!

Avoiding things that remind you of a past traumatic event. You may try to avoid certain people or situations that remind you of the event. For example, someone who was assaulted on the bus might avoid taking public transportation, or a combat veteran may avoid crowded places like shopping malls because it feels dangerous to be around so many people. You may also try to stay busy all the time so you don't have to talk or think about the event.

Prevention Is the Key!

Call the VA or a local vet center directly. They have "been there" and "done that"! The VA can help you understand the standard treatments and the treatment options available for veterans. Veteran's service organizations (VSOs) such as the VFW, Disabled American Veterans (DAV), and American Legion, among others can help you get your benefits and file for benefits on your behalf, greatly easing the burden of trying to file directly online yourself. These organizations provide free assistance and follow-up with the VA.

This is your day! History does repeat itself, and your education, experience(s), and repetitive response(s) have led you to today! Work with your immediate family, friends, therapists, and doctors to cope. Become a student of your experiences, and recognize and be thankful that there is another day, for you can make a difference! Seek HELP for your *stressors*.

One Day at a Time!

W.S. Wright

I am now in my seventies, having completed 42 years in the US Marine Corps as an aviator and Marine. As I begin to rest and enjoy a slower pace, I reflect the many training sessions, exercises, deployments, TDYs, unaccompanied tours, episodes, memories, and flights that I would never had seen had I not been a naval aviator, fighter pilot (F-4B, F-4J, F-4N, F-4S and F-4-Blue Angel Conf.), squadron maintenance pilot, close air support pilot (A-4M, TA-4J, F-4B, F-4J, and F-4N), and an engineering test pilot flying various systems evaluations.

To reflect on how I got to my age, I can only think of the many stressors that I experienced in my lifetime and how different the military situations can be. The basis of my response and reactions all begin in the same foundation, developed in a similar environment, yet I reacted and responded differently on the outcome since that outcome was strongly influenced by the final interaction and result.

Consider when driving down the highway at 60 mph. You are actually traveling at 88 feet per second. Now that's like going down a football field at 30 yards a second! Well, the naval aviator flies twice that fast to land, three times faster than that below 10,000 ft, and tactically six times that speed not to mention all naval aviation, sea, and tactics on teamwork and being close to your "dive buddy." So when the Blue Angels fly by in the diamond formation at 450 knots with wing overlap, build just 3 feet from your "bud's" canopy. Formation flying is critical and the attention to detail is pressing and a necessity! I learned that early, right after solo, nav, and carrier landing practice.

Now, we began to launch with another F9F for weapons and tactics demo training. One morning, the section (2 flight instructors, 2 student flight aviators, and 2 F9F aircraft) had just finished the 45-minute training mission, and we were RTB. I was on the lead's right wing and practicing turns and "crossunders" but not good enough! "Lieutenant, you are not in position! Drive the nose of the aircraft into position on the starboard side like you're a Blue Angel flying ready for a high-speed pass on the tower!"

(Work it!)
(Work it!)
(Work it!)
(Work it!)

"No, lieutenant! Got to be closer! And don't worry about the flight path! This old Cougar jet can take quite a beating! Move that stick and throttle like you are killing rats! There's enough energy. Go 'full up!' a long time before the engine will catch up!"

"I got it! Let me show you, and then you'll be in position to fly high and tight just like the Blue Angels!"

(Work it!)
(Work it!)
(Work it!)

He worked it, and we were "high and tight." We were high and tight and closer than the blues! I could hear the instructor pilot smiling from tear to ear that he got his chance to show me how to be there and be high and tight again *except* our flight path is fast tracking toward the landing pattern, and we were so close and "tucked in" and under the lead's fuselage. Neither the instructor pilot nor I saw lead's hand signal that he was going to "straighten out" and enter the "overhead" for the "break downwind and (uneventful) landing."

Yep! It happened! Lead's wing tip struck the windscreen and broke the plexiglass canopy! As a result of the impact, the inside of the cockpit was quickly cleaned of all maps, flight logs, helmet bags, and other loose equipment quickly. After all, we were now flying around in an open-air F9F Cougar at 250 knots.

Good news! Aircraft had no flight control problems. However the instructor pilot had been stuck by a piece of the canopy and his ICS and radio connection had disengaged on impact! He was alarmed, confused, bleeding, and shaking the stick I yelled, "I got it!! I got it!! I got it!!" Pilot command was passed, and Tempest 212 landed uneventfully and stopped on the 6/24 apron to meet the crash crew and ambulance for the instructor pilot. Once released by the emergency crew, I taxied to the flight line and checked in and debriefed the AMO and air ops duty officer. Glad to be back on terra firma with another chance to demonstrate my education and training, recognize the life-threatening stressors, and go for one day at a time!

There was a time that I got outstanding for handling emergency procedure and below average for formation flying. It took me a while to get into high and tight, "closer than the blues," and move that stick and throttle like you are killing rats, but I did and I became a naval aviator on August 13, 1968. One day at a time!

During ACM practice with an "experienced" squadron section leader, we got into a slow speed scissors in our F-4Js over an undercast sky. I worked my aircraft into a "Fox one" position and pressed for a "Guns" run, low on energy and fuel yet pressing for the right guns position. I stalled the aircraft close to 250 knots and "broke it off" just as I got to "Bingo" fuel, the ACM 10,000 ft. ceiling and the top of the undercast sky while recovering from an approach turn stall. At that time, we were only 75 miles (19 minutes) from the IAF and 45 miles (12 minutes) from the DMZ as we turned for an uneventful, timely straight in, on speed, "on ball" approach, and landing. One day at a time!

During a combat support flight in Vietnam, Sandy 01 (FAC) was marking a 23mm gun position for Covey 239 when he was shot down by this position. Covey 239 pinpointed that position, and he immediately called for air support. Sabre 211 and Tempest 212, a section of F-4s, responded with 500 lb. bombs and 20mm guns. While the FAC was marking the enemy gun position, he received ground fire from the twin-barrel 23mm gun positions that were 30 meters apart. Sabre and Tempest began their attacks while receiving ground fire from both 23mm gun positions. On the second pass, the ground fire was more intense and the flight delivered their ordnance on target in spite of the ground fire. There was an immediate secondary explosion at one 23mm, silencing the other position for approximately 45 minutes. We can assume that the second gun crew had been killed. This effort to recover the downed FAC, Sandy 01, continued for two days, and more than six aircraft were shot down and nine aircrew members were on the ground. The second day, Sabre and Tempest were ready to get back on target and assist with the aircrew recovery. We were on target more than 1.2 hours again to reap damage and assist in the aircrew recovery.

These two days in April 1970 will long be remembered by many. A great deal of US Air Force and Marine Corps airpower was brought to bear against a heavy concentration of enemy antiaircraft gun sites in support of the SAR effort of Hostage Man and Cowpoke 18. The courage, accuracy, and determination of Sabre 211, Tempest 212, and other fighter aircraft to deliver timely and accurate ordnance in the face of heavy and accurate antiaircraft fire demonstrated an extremely professional effort. Only one aircrew was lost (possibly on a late, low-altitude helicopter departure), and the NVA never used that gun site again! One day at a time!

Biography of W.S. Wright

I am now in my 70's, after completing 42 years in the US Marine Corps as an aviator and Marine. As I began to rest and enjoy a slower pace, I reflected the many training sessions, CommXs, deployments, TDYs, unaccompanied tours, episodes, memories, and flights that I would never had seen had I not been a naval aviator, fighter pilot (F-4B, F-4J, F4N, F-4S, and F-4 Blue Angel Conf.), squadron maintenance pilot, close air support pilot (A-4M, TA-4J, F-4B, F-4J, and F-4N), engineering test pilot—various systems evaluation(s), military training and education (OCS, USAFA, USN Naval Aviator, USMC TBS, USMC AWS, USA Test Pilot School, USMC Command and Staff College, and US Army War College).

My formal education past high school was at the University of Michigan (BSE aero)—Ann Arbor, Miami, University of Southern California (MS Systems)—Los Angeles, California, and Claremont Graduate School (Executive MBA)—Claremont, California. To reflect on how I got to my age, I can only think of the many stressors that I experienced and coped with in my lifetime and how different the military situations can be.

W.S. (Stan) Wright flew 200 combat missions and received 2 distinguished flying crosses, 11 air medals, and the navy commendation medal for his service and gallantry in Vietnam. He retired from the Corps at the rank major.

Anxiety

Overview

It is natural to worry and feel anxious about things—that presentation at work, your growing to-do list, a relationship. Anxiety can help you confront stresses in your life, and for many people, the feeling is motivating and doesn't last long. But when persistent worries start affecting your day-to-day activities, your work, your sleep, or your relationships, it may be time to do something about it.

Anxiety problems are common and uncomfortable. Almost one-third of adults will experience some form of distressing anxiety at some point in their lifetime. Symptoms can include:

- feeling restless, jumpy, or on edge
- excessive worrying about everyday decisions
- difficulty concentrating
- a racing heart or cold, clammy hands
- trembling or twitching
- having trouble catching your breath
- feeling dizzy, nauseous, or light-headed
- difficulty sleeping

The good news is that there are effective treatment options for overcoming problems with anxiety.

Social anxiety

Most people feel anxious in some social situations sometimes, but for people with social phobia, that anxiety is strong and long-lasting. Social phobia can keep people from doing things they want to do, such as public speaking or attending a crowded event like a concert or a football game.

Generalized anxiety

People with generalized anxiety feel as if they're always worried or anxious about a range of things in their daily lives. They have trouble controlling or stopping these worries whether they are about work, school, money, relationships, or their health.
People with generalized anxiety sometimes describe themselves as "worrywarts" and are often told that they worry too much. They may also experience symptoms of tension, including restlessness, quick exhaustion, difficulty in concentrating, irritability, muscle tension, sleep difficulties, and inability to relax.

Panic attacks

People with panic disorder have recurrent, unexpected episodes of intense fear or discomfort called panic attacks. A panic attack is accompanied by symptoms such as heart palpitations, difficulty breathing, a racing or pounding heart, trembling, chest pain, stomach distress, dizziness or light-headedness, and numbing or tingling. During a panic attack, people often feel afraid that they are out of control or even that their life is at risk.

Although most people experience a panic attack at some point, those with panic disorder worry about having more panic attacks and will often do things to try to prevent them. They might avoid situations that are difficult to leave, such as a client meeting or concert, because they fear having a panic attack. This can significantly limit a person's ability to experience and enjoy life. When people avoid situations because they are afraid, they will have a panic attack, or they may be experiencing panic disorder with agoraphobia.

Specific phobias

A person with a specific phobia experiences intense fear in response to a particular object or situation. For example, fear of blood or needles, of enclosed places, and of flying are common specific phobias.

Sometimes specific phobias arise or become more of an issue after a person relocates to an area with a higher risk of encountering what they fear. For example, if someone has a specific phobia of earthquakes, that fear may intensify after moving from Chicago to Los Angeles, where earthquakes are common. The key to coping with these phobias is recognizing when they are getting in the way of your everyday life.

Source: https://www.mentalhealth.va.gov/mentalhealth/anxiety/index.asp. (The site offers screening checklists to aid in identifying the anxiety topics discussed above.)

My to-do list for today:

-Count my blessings
-Practice kindness
-Let go of what I can't control
-Listen to my heart
-Be productive yet calm
-Just breathe

From Teenager to Manhood in Less Than a Year

John Young

I was sworn into the United States Army on my 19th birthday at Fort Jackson, SC. After completing my basic training, I next went to Fort Gordon, Georgia for 9 weeks of airborne infantry training followed by jump school. After 30 days' leave in September 1968, I was Vietnam bound in October and was assigned to the American division as an infantryman. I had an upsetting few moments when I was MIA after action on January 10, 1969, but I was eventually rejoined with my unit. On January 15, 1969, I was wounded in action and received the Purple Heart and a Bronze Star, and I rejoined my unit after convalescing. In July, I became ill like many of us did, thinking it was malaria. The diagnosis was hepatitis C, and I spent 12 weeks in Tokyo recuperating. The war was over for me. When I got back to the US, the first thing I did was kiss the ground. I was so thankful to be back.

Not everyone who went to Vietnam got to come back; they gave their all. The things I saw and heard in Vietnam left me with a lot of problems. Coming back, I had to settle with the Lord that I had taken someone's life. I never heard of PTSD until the effects of what I experienced over many years started filtering into my life with greater frequency and intensity. I tried different things to get help including one-on-one counseling. A counselor told me to try a combat peer support group. That changed everything. There is simply nothing like it. The group has helped each person in some way. I experienced a low point when my wife of 42 years passed away; I felt a great sense of loss. It was tremendous help to me when members of the group checked on me to be sure I was okay and see if I needed anything. Everyone in the group has a "specialness" about him, and we have a bond. I've learned that participating in the group sessions and staying in contact with one another is important in the recovery and support process.

Bubba Bowie

Michael Hunt

I joined the Army in 1989 and primarily served as a machine gunner for three years. I completed approximately 30 combat missions during operations Just Cause, Promote Liberty, and Garden Plot. I served as an assistant crew chief and door gunner during the Persian Gulf War. Lastly, I worked as a Department of Defense contractor during operations Iraqi Freedom and Enduring Freedom.

My first service-related emotional breakdown occurred while serving on a funeral detail in the spring of 1991 when we buried a number of soldiers and veterans in the National Cemetery at Riverside, California. The next experience occurred while attending a combat leadership course, which was demanding and stressful. Soon after this, I began drinking and having relationship problems, which led to suicidal thoughts. My next training assignment at Twentynine Palms, California produced more emotional stress for me. Another funeral detail assignment in 1993 produced an emotional breakdown, and I went AWOL. I received an Article 15 and was reduced in rank by one grade. I was referred to the hospital at Fort Ord, California, treated, and released for suicidal ideation. The staff referred me to a chaplain for counseling, which I completed. I tested for the Expert Infantryman Badge (EIB), however the resulting emotional stress inside me was overwhelming so that I did not complete the qualification. I was subsequently not allowed to reenlist and was honorably discharged in 1993.

My wife and I started having marital problems. I was drinking heavily and started gambling, which gave me the adrenaline "rush" that I lacked after service. The local police were called out to our home three times for domestic violence though I was never charged. After the third incident, I left my wife and moved back to Louisiana where I became a truck driver. I have held 26 jobs, including owning and operating 3 small businesses that failed. In the past twenty-six years I have been out of the army, I have been unemployed for more than five years. I realized I could not hold a job or maintain a healthy relationship for any length of time. My family and friends had given up on me.

I didn't care if I lived or died. They told me that something was wrong and that I needed help, but I was in denial.

When the Iraq War started in 2003, I was recruited as a Department of Defense contractor in October. After four months of 100-hour work weeks and approximately 60 missions, I had another emotional breakdown in March 2004 and resigned. In May 2004, the DOD recruited me to be a classified courier based in Turkey. I was there for a short time and experienced a blackout, which resulted in hospitalization. I was diagnosed with PTSD and bipolar depression. I was in complete denial, but I took my medications until I recovered enough to return to work. In September 2004, I went back to work as a truck driver for six months until I fell asleep at the wheel, causing me to realize it was time to get off the road. I quit, packed my bags, and moved to Florida with the intention of living it up until the money ran out and then killing myself. In May 2005, I attempted suicide by taking a bottle of Risperdal pills and alcohol.

In June 2005, a friend of mine convinced me to come to the VA for help. I went to the ER, and even though I was a combat veteran, they denied me treatment. The VA maintained I could not receive treatment because I had no insurance and made too much money the year prior. They referred me to the Tampa Vet Center, which informed me that I need to see a psychiatrist and get back on my meds. The downside was a six-month wait to get the psych appointment. Next, they suggested I get a job and some insurance. In December 2005, I was driving a truck and blacked out behind the wheel, running off the road. I was arrested for DUI, but the charges were dropped because I had not been drinking and was in a psychotic state. I was jailed. I could not function or make decisions for myself. I had the money to post bail but had no idea who I was or what I was doing in jail. The police kept me in solitary for 3–4 weeks because they determined I was incompetent and a danger to myself or others. When I was finally allowed to post bail, a friend took me to the Tampa Vet Center, which got me a bed in the psych ward at the VA hospital, the date being January 2006.

My symptoms related to PTSD caused by combat stressors include, but are not limited to, suicidal ideation, homicidal ideation, violent outbursts, severe panic attacks, delusions, anxiety attacks, recurring nightmares, intrusive thoughts and memories, flashbacks, sleep disturbances, hypersomnia, appetite disturbances, isolation, frequent crying episodes without knowing the precipitants, and increased anxiety hypervigilance.

My emotional breakdowns, suicidal thoughts, homicidal ideation, and violent outbursts became progressively worse from 1991 up to my final disassociation blackout in 2005. Since being hospitalized for PTSD due to combat stressors, I have done my best to work hard on my recovery. I have complied with everything the doctors and case managers have asked me to do, and I am medication compliant. Yet the disabling symptoms I suffer from are still keeping me from working, getting vocational rehabilitation training, and developing and maintaining healthy relationships. My Global Assessment of

Functioning (GAF) score has dropped from 52 to 39. My delusions have become worse.

Since my work attempt in October 2009 failed due to severe panic attacks and other stress-related symptoms, I have boxed myself in. I never leave my apartment except to go to the VA, the St. Petersburg Vet Center, and the grocery store just steps from my apartment. Unless accompanied by my roommate or a case manager. I frequently can't sleep at night due to panic attacks. Frequently I have anxiety attacks while eating or watching TV. The more stressed I am, the worse my intrusive thoughts are, which triggers hypervigilance reactions. I remember a lot of codes and numbers associated with combat missions, and sometimes hearing just a fragment of a code or call sign will cause my hypervigilance to flare up.

Like Fleas on a Hound Dog

Willie Spurlin

I lived in Baton Rouge when the deadly Louisiana flood occurred in August 2016. It was this flood that led to my Vietnam flashback. I served in the navy in Vietnam from 1968–1972. I was on river patrol operating from the USS *Vancouver*. My duties included loading supplies and transporting Marines up and down the river to get them relief. We fell under heavy fire several times. Part of my job included retrieving dead bodies. Imagine that. An 18-year-old young man who hadn't had the opportunity to be an adult yet, pulling dead bodies out of the water, fearing all the time he would end up like one of them. Those memories are ingrained into my very being, which largely contributed to me developing PTSD.

After Vietnam, I became a truck driver and ended up driving 18-wheelers for 30 years. Once I retired, my PTSD became more noticeable to my loved ones. Since I was no longer working 80 hours per week and on the road all the time, I became more and more antsy. I couldn't tolerate being in crowds or going places like movie theaters or restaurants. If I was out and saw someone wearing black, I would go to other side of parking lot. And everywhere I went, I was always checking the perimeter. My family was frightened for me.

Then came the August 2016 flood. It rained 50+ inches straight without stopping. Streets were completely flooded. Rescue boats were out, and there were helicopters flying overhead. It looked like a war zone. All of this was what brought on my flashback. When the sheriff found me, I was crawling through the mud on my stomach and holding my arms like I had gun.

Soon after, I went to see the doctor, and she helped me to get settled down with medication. She recommended I go to a combat peer support group. I ended up going to a group meeting, and from the moment I walked through the door the first day, "Charlie Brown" (Chuck Wright), "Catfish" (John Young), and "Web-Foot" (John Reynolds) put me under their wing. I was still very hyper, but I didn't feel like they held it against me. The group was there to talk to me when I needed to talk, and I got comfortable with them, which is hard to do with PTSD. Charlie Brown would not give up on me. We'd go to breakfast once or twice a week as a way to keep in contact. They kept me grounded, and I looked forward to going to the group. I know that I can count on them to call and check on me. They stuck on me like fleas on a hound dog! It's hard for anyone with PTSD to get a friend, but they didn't judge me. Without the peer support group and without the support of good friends, I would not be as good as I am today. It's also helped me to give back to others as a volunteer at my VA clinic. I call people to remind them of their appointments, direct people where they need to go when they come inside, and help other volunteers if they need wheelchairs. Giving back keeps you from getting locked inside of your own mind. You must give your time and energy and care to someone else instead of using those negative factors feed your PTSD.

Lightning and thunder are my worst triggers. During those times, I huddle together with my two dogs and my wife, and we wait out the storm. Every night, I have nightmares, and my legs don't stop moving. I take medication, which helps me sleep at night. And I hold on to my wife, Diane; she's my anchor.

No One Heals Alone

Joshua Clark

No one heals alone. These are words that I live by daily now as a Marine and a soon-to-be veteran. Coming from the Corps and the infantry I never knew how PTSD could affect an individual. I had the assumption that as a salty grunt I was going to be emotionally bullet-proof, having a handle on life, and every situation that would get thrown down range at me. I was mistaken. Most of the time I have learned that it sneaks up on you in subtle ways, but it is lethal. You really cannot see it coming, as it grabs you at your weakest moments and seemingly sucks the absolute life out of you.

For me, my struggle and suffering birthed itself from ways that were not particularly combat related, which is why I avoided it altogether for so long. I think that is a large misconception with many of the veterans I work with today on healing. Truth be told, I have lost 5 members I have served with from suicide and an additional 2 from alcoholism. The common denominator was that not one of us served in combat. In 2013, I arrived in the Fleet Marine Force eager to serve my country and create a legacy.

My unit had just returned from Afghanistan, and it had been rumored we were preparing for a workup for Syria. To expedite the timeline of events, we ended up doing a bland deployment to Japan where I first experienced alcoholism. It became a way for me to pass the time. I was bored and felt like a caged dog waiting to be let loose. My son's biological mother was pregnant for the second time, the first ending in a miscarriage while I was at recruit training. I believe the stressors I felt—being away from home, not being there for the pregnancy, not knowing what my future held overseas or if my son would make it—was more than I could cope with. I still had to hold myself above the standard as a Marine and prepare for a war day in and out. This was the beginning stages of my ultimate downfall.

Soon after coming home from deployment, I met my son and was promoted to the rank of sergeant. In a time where I had to lead by example and absorb the problems of an entire platoon, it was when my key leadership was leaving. I was focusing the majority on my time on my Marines and their well-being. I found myself in the midst of a broken marriage, battered by adultery with another Marine involving my ex-wife. The pressure to perform at work and have it all together as the polished and poised Sergeant Clark mixed with the stressors of a broken marriage at home and the pretense to my family that I had it together while staying in a toxic environment led to more unhealthy coping mechanisms. I went into a deep depression, became addicted to alcohol, and had zero self-worth with nowhere to go with my emotions. Along the way, I knew I was straying further and further away from my life with Jesus Christ. I was raised in a wonderful, godly household, and my parents were as good as they come. I knew the right way to go about things, but thinking and doing are polar opposites. My closest Marine friends and I finally went separate ways with reassignments, reenlistments, and end of tours shortly after my son's mother moved him back to Texas. A week later, I received a phone call that one of my closest friends had been killed in Oklahoma. He was a mentor for me. A Marine I served with committed suicide, and to top it off, my son was diagnosed with autism at the age two. Again, I found myself alone.

Coming home, the friends I once had no longer understood me nor I them. Four years aged me twelve years mentally and emotionally. Things we see and do as military members on a daily basis are not easily understood. So much was going south for me. I was divorced and broke. I rarely saw my child with special needs and was in an uncivil relationship with his mother. My career performance disturbed me. I felt I was not doing enough for my country. I was alone, depressed, angry, and confused on how to heal. My highlight each day was to see how much liquor was in my refrigerator at seven each evening.

I had cut myself off from family and friends. All I knew how to do was work for the corps, get blasted, wake up sober, and repeat the process. I was spiraling out of control and losing friends I had served with to suicide. I was falling into a darker place time after time. Finally, I got my wake-up call one evening when I blacked out in my apartment with a loaded pistol next to my head, its safety off. My eyes were glaring down the barrel.

At that point, I realized the only thing who would take care of me was God as He had done before. I knew if I was this broken, there were plenty of other veterans out there needing assistance. I stood by my corps values as a Marine and translated them into my daily life and Christian life. I knew that there was more to me besides despair and that I would be the loaded weapon for the world to heal. I had all the tools to make a difference and create a life worth following for my son, peers, and ultimately you who are reading this.

Since giving my life back to Jesus Christ, I was blessed with my wife and soul mate. I have a family of three and became an ordained military veteran chaplain. I am still going strong as a Marine on active duty. My son and family are thriving depression-free. My healing is ongoing, and I hope if you gain anything out of this, it's just that. My way of healing is serving those who have served. It's okay to not be okay. But as men and women above reproach, we must take a stand against PTSD. It is the enemy, and we must maintain a "kill or be killed" mentality. You have all the makings to be exceptional and overcome any obstacle. Look yourself in the mirror, remember where you came from, and take the fight to the fight. If you're suffering, it's because the enemy knows your strengths. God knows your potential, and you still are called to serve in some capacity on this earth. Good luck! I'm praying for you. *Rah!*

Joshua Clark Biography

Joshua Clark served four years in the United States Marine Corps in the infantry as a mortarman with 3d Light Armored Reconnaissance Battalion in Twentynine Palms, California, and is still currently serving on active duty until 2021. He works also as a crisis responder for suicide prevention and is a certified PTSD counselor. He serves as director of operations for the Birdwell Foundation (a nonprofit organization combatting PTSD and veteran and first responder suicide) in Houston, Texas.

Self-Care and Coping with PTSD Effects

It is common to experience some level of stress reactions after a trauma. Many people feel detached or down, have sleep problems and nightmares, or have flashbacks where they feel the event is happening again. How people respond to these normal reactions may make the difference between long-lasting symptoms and short-lived problems.

If you have PTSD or have symptoms that last longer than a few months after the traumatic event is over, your best chance of getting better is by working with a mental health or medical provider. Good treatments are available and have been shown to help all kinds of people. If you continue to experience distress, see a mental health or medical provider. Talking to your primary care provider is a good place to start.

When those who have been through trauma take direct action to cope with their stress reactions, they put themselves in a position of power. For people who have completed therapy for PTSD, practicing coping skills helps manage symptoms that can arise due to triggers or new stress. Learn about healthy coping strategies that you can use after a trauma or for continued self-care.

Active coping

Active coping means accepting the impact of trauma on your life and taking direct action to improve things. Active coping occurs even when there is no crisis. Active coping is a way of responding to everyday life. It is a habit that must be made stronger.

Know that recovery is a process

Following exposure to a trauma, most people experience stress reactions. Understand that recovering from the trauma is a process and takes time. Knowing this will help you feel more in control.

- Having an ongoing response to the trauma is normal.
- Recovery is an ongoing, daily process. It happens little by little. It is not a matter of being cured immediately.
- Healing doesn't mean forgetting traumatic events. It doesn't mean you will have no pain or bad feelings when thinking about them.
- Healing may mean fewer symptoms and symptoms that bother you less.
- Healing means more confidence that you will be able to cope with your memories and symptoms. You will be better able to manage your feelings.

Positive Coping Reactions

Certain actions can help reduce your distressing symptoms and make things better. Plus these actions can result in changes that last into the future. Here are some positive coping methods.

Learn about trauma and PTSD

It is useful for trauma survivors to learn more about common reactions to trauma and about PTSD. Find out what is normal. Find out what the signs are that you may need assistance from others. When you learn that the symptoms of PTSD are common, you realize that you are not alone, weak, or crazy. It helps to know your problems are shared by hundreds of thousands of others. When you seek treatment and begin to understand your response to trauma, you will be better able to cope with the symptoms of PTSD.

Talk to others for support

When survivors talk about their problems with others, something helpful often results. It is important not to isolate yourself. Instead make efforts to be with others. Of course, you must choose your support people with care. You must also ask them clearly for what you need. With support from others, you may feel less alone and more understood. You may also get concrete help with a problem you have.

Practice relaxation methods

Try some different ways to relax, including:

- exercising for muscle relaxation
- breathing exercises
- meditating
- swimming, stretching, doing yoga
- praying
- listening to quiet music
- spending time in nature

While relaxation techniques can be helpful, to a few people, they can sometimes increase distress at first. This can happen when you focus attention on disturbing physical sensations and you reduce contact with the outside world. Most often, continuing with relaxation in small amounts that you can handle will help reduce negative reactions. You may want to try mixing relaxation in with music, walking, or other activities.

Distract yourself with positive activities

Pleasant recreational or work activities help distract a person from his or her memories and reactions. For example, art has been a way for many trauma survivors to express their feelings in a positive, creative way. Pleasant activities can improve your mood, limit the harm caused by PTSD, and help you rebuild your life.

Talking to your doctor or a counselor about trauma and PTSD

Part of taking care of yourself means using the helping resources around you. If efforts at coping don't seem to work, you may become fearful or depressed. If your PTSD symptoms don't begin to go away or get worse over time, it is important to reach out and call a counselor who can help turn things around. Your family doctor can also refer you to a specialist who can treat PTSD. Talk to your doctor about your trauma and your PTSD symptoms. That way, he or she can take care of your health better.

Many with PTSD have found treatment with medicines to be helpful for some symptoms. By taking medicines, some survivors of trauma are able to improve their sleep, anxiety, irritability, and anger. It can also reduce urges to drink or use drugs.

Coping with the Symptoms of PTSD

Here are some direct ways to cope with these specific PTSD symptoms.

Unwanted distressing memories, images, or thoughts

- Remind yourself that they are just that. Memories.
- Remind yourself that it's natural to have some memories of the trauma(s).
- Talk about them with someone you trust.
- Remember that although reminders of trauma can feel overwhelming, they often lessen with time.

Sudden feelings of anxiety or panic

Traumatic stress reactions often include feeling your heart pounding and feeling light-headed or spacey. This is usually caused by rapid breathing. If this happens, remember that

- these reactions are not dangerous. If you had them while exercising, they most likely would not worry you.
- these feelings often come with scary thoughts that are not true. For example, you may think, "I'm going to die," "I'm having a heart attack," or "I will lose control." It is the scary thoughts that make these reactions so upsetting.
- slowing down your breathing may help.
- the sensations will pass soon and then you can go on with what you were doing.

Each time you respond in these positive ways to your anxiety or panic, you will be working toward making it happen less often. Practice will make it easier to cope.

Feeling like the trauma is happening again (flashbacks)

- Keep your eyes open. Look around you and notice where you are.
- Talk to yourself. Remind yourself where you are, what year you're in, and that you are safe. The trauma happened in the past, and you are in the present.
- Get up and move around. Have a drink of water and wash your hands.
- Call someone you trust and tell them what is happening.
- Remind yourself that this is a common response after trauma.
- Tell your counselor or doctor about the flashback(s).

Dreams and nightmares related to the trauma

- If you wake up from a nightmare in a panic, remind yourself that you are reacting to a dream. Having the dream is why you are in a panic, not because there is real danger now.
- You may want to get up out of bed, regroup, and orient yourself to the here and now.
- Engage in a pleasant, calming activity. For example, listen to some soothing music.
- Talk to someone if possible.
- Talk to your doctor about your nightmares. Certain medicines can be helpful.

Difficulty falling or staying asleep

- Keep to a regular bedtime schedule.
- Avoid heavy exercise for the few hours just before going to bed.

- Avoid using your sleeping area for anything other than sleeping or sex.
- Avoid alcohol, tobacco, and caffeine. These harm your ability to sleep.
- Do not lie in bed thinking or worrying. Get up and enjoy something soothing or pleasant. Read a calming book, drink a glass of warm milk or herbal tea, or do a quiet hobby.

Irritability, anger, and rage

- Take a time out to cool off or think things over. Walk away from the situation.
- Get in the habit of exercising daily. Exercise reduces body tension and relieves stress.
- Remember that staying angry doesn't work. It actually increases your stress and can cause additional health problems.
- Talk to your counselor or doctor about your anger. Take classes on how to manage anger.
- If you blow up at family members or friends, find time as soon as you can to talk to them about it. Let them know how you feel and what you are doing to cope with your reactions.

Difficulty concentrating or staying focused

- Slow down. Give yourself time to focus on what it is you need to learn or do.
- Write things down. Making to-do lists may be helpful.
- Break tasks down into doable small chunks.
- Plan a realistic number of events or tasks for each day.

- You may be depressed. Many people who are depressed have trouble concentrating. Again, this is something you can discuss with your counselor, doctor, or someone close to you.

Trouble feeling or expressing positive emotions

- Remember that this is a common reaction to trauma. You are not doing this on purpose. You should not feel guilty for something you do not want to happen and cannot control.
- Make sure to keep taking part in activities that you enjoy or used to enjoy. Even if you don't think you will enjoy something, once you get into it, you may well start having feelings of pleasure.
- Take steps to let your loved ones know that you care. You can express your caring in little ways: write a card, leave a small gift, or phone someone and say hello.

A Final Word

Try using all these ways of coping to find which ones are helpful to you. Then *practice* them. Like other skills, they work better with practice. Be aware that there are also behaviors that *don't* help.
Source: www.ptsd.va.gov

> **BE KIND.**
> FOR EVERYONE YOU MEET IS FIGHTING A BATTLE YOU KNOW NOTHING ABOUT.

Grateful for My Comrades

Ron "Rabbit" Clark

I was born and raised in Iowa, just a simple country boy growing up on a farm. When I turned eighteen, I voluntarily enlisted into the navy. The fact of the matter was my draft number was fourteen, so I knew my turn would come up sooner rather than later. I chose the navy because I like water and figured I could see different parts of the world. It wasn't until I was headed out on a ship that we were told we were going to Vietnam. I thought to myself, *Oh, great! Just what I need!*

I served in Vietnam from 1968 to 1972. The Navy wanted me to be a medic, and I said, "No way. The medics and radiomen were the first to get killed." So I served as part of the assault group task force. We took supplies and Marines up and down the river.

When I came back from Vietnam, I was stationed in San Diego. One day, I was walking on the beach, enjoying the sunshine, when I heard a guy yelling at me.

"Baby killer!" he screamed.

"What did you just say?" I asked him in disbelief.

"Over in Vietnam, you were killing women and children and babies," he said.

I looked at him straight in the eyes and said, "If I had a gun and you had a gun, and I was pointing my gun at you, what are you going to do?"

The guy responded, "Well, I'd shoot you."

I told him, "Well, there you go."

When I got back to Iowa, my first doctor didn't know anything about PTSD. He put me on antidepressants and anti-anxiety meds. I started drinking a lot—a cooler of beer when I went to work and one when I got home. My marriage was not a happy one. But still, I thought I was a normal person.

I moved to Texas in 2013 to be with family and for medical reasons. I felt I needed to talk to someone, so I went to a VA psychologist and was told I didn't have PTSD. I learned about various support groups centered around PTSD. I thought they were crazy, not knowing what PTSD was. Comrades recommended going to a peer group. I was apprehensive because I thought PTSD was a joke.

Charlie Brown introduced me to the combat peer support group I am a part of now. Listening to other brothers talk about the experiences they had in combat… It all just gelled together. I understood more about the effects of my PTSD. I am grateful for my comrades because they helped me get my life straightened out.

Observations on My Vietnam Experience

Delta 56

I was commissioned a second lieutenant, infantry at Fort Benning, Georgia in August 1968. After graduation, I had a short assignment in Maryland and then departed for some advanced infantry schools before going to Vietnam. I went over, well trained and prepared for my tour, trying to be confident in my abilities as a platoon leader.

After about eight days of in processing and orientation, I was eventually assigned to a unit in IV Corps, the southernmost operating area also known as the Mekong Delta. I interviewed with the brigade commander who gave me the gung ho "body count" metrics talk. "We need bodies to show mission success!" I met my battalion and company commanders the next morning and got my platoon assignment.

The delta terrain was flat, hot, filthy, and wet with canals and creeks running everywhere. It was a miserable environment, especially in the monsoon season. I was twenty-three years old at this time. Most of the guys in my platoon were 19–20 years old, so early on, I became the "old man." The lieutenant I replaced had been wounded and rotated back home. My platoon sergeant had about three months in the field with this platoon and was one of the "more experienced" members. The other platoon members were less experienced due to losses and rotations of newbies into the platoon. I depended on him a lot to do the job.

My platoon mostly conducted security patrols for 2–3 days from a firebase near division headquarters, generally no more than 10–15 kilometers from that location. Our mission was to protect the division headquarters. Typically, we would return to base, stand down for a couple of days, and do it all over again. Other times, we would participate in numerous airmobile operations as part of a larger force, typically hitting three to four targets, patrolling, and attempting to establish contact with a Vietcong (VC) force. These missions sometimes went on for several days if we were part of a larger operation.

I can still recall one of my first initial contacts with a VC force while we were on patrol. Luckily, they were somehow caught by surprise, and we had them boxed in quickly. I called in artillery and mortars on their position in an attempt to disperse them into the open or kill them in place. After the artillery ceased, we mopped up. The horror of what we had done became indelibly etched in my mind. As kids, my buddies and I watched black-and-white war movies with relish and played war games. This was nothing like that! It was Technicolor, and it had smells and horrible noises. It was carnage I had never imagined. The damage on human targets was obscene. Army training did not prepare me for that. I still have recurring dreams of that first contact on some occasions though less frequently now.

By 1969, making enemy contact and engaging them was hard to do. The VC knew that US forces were leaving when drawdowns were announced, and they knew they could defeat the Army of Vietnam (ARVN) forces. The VC were in no hurry to waste their own lives unnecessarily. "Be patient and wait" was their order of the day. A war of attrition ensued against us. It chewed away at us. They resorted to using more booby traps and the occasional snipers on a vastly larger scale. Most of my platoon's casualties, to include myself, were from booby traps (now referred to as IEDs). The routine days of patrols without contact tempered with booby traps in many places that wore us down. We just wanted to stay alive and go home. My platoon's casualties disturbed me deeply and still do to this day. As a body of men, we were literally raw with anger and frustration trying to confront an enemy that wouldn't engage. We frequently treated civilians harshly for being perceived as VC agents and sympathizers. Our brutality on these people is another disturbing series of events I brought home with me.

Exactly fifty years ago as I write this, I was among the first 25,000 personnel to be pulled out of Vietnam around the end of August 1969. Our brigade was selected as one of the units to return in the drawdown of forces. Many of us went to Hawaii, which was admittedly a nice place to decompress. I was there only a month and assigned the HQ shop to conduct inventories at the dock when containers of sensitive equipment arrived (weapons, commo gear, crypto equipment typically). Each identified container needed to be accounted for and documented so the contents could be forwarded for reissue or maintenance. At the end of this month or so, I returned to the mainland to finish my remaining service obligation.

Returning home, I was unprepared for the reactions I encountered from civilians. I was never spat on, but I did sense some of the "baby killer" hostility in their glances or stares at the airport in San Francisco where I landed. Civilians were not happy with US policy in Vietnam. I was angry with that. Future encounters sometimes ended with words or worse. Eventually, I refused to even talk about serving in Vietnam to avoid punching out people I didn't really care about.

I was assigned to a military unit near Fort Ord, California. The duty was great, and seeing my fiancée again took the edge off and helped me settle down. She never asked me much about my time in Vietnam, and I never volunteered much.

After we married a few months later, we had to explore options for our future—go to graduate school, extend in the army, or find a job. Graduate school was out; I wasn't ready for academics again. If I were to extend in the army, I would be promoted to captain and sent off for advanced army schooling and back to Vietnam. That was not going to happen. I began the job search. I got job interviews. All inevitably asked what I did in Vietnam, and those interviews chilled quickly when I discussed the intricacies of closing with and destroying the enemy. I quickly learned to lie about Vietnam and fabricated my role as an assistant supply officer or some administrative officer. After literally dozens of interviews, I finally got a job offer. Ironically, the personnel manager who made the job offer was a recently separated navy aviator who flew off carriers off Vietnam.

The quality of life from my collective Vietnam experiences plateaued; it wasn't getting better or worse. The nightmares and anxiety attacks were occurring frequently. I know the experiences and reactions probably rattled my wife and children later on, but I wouldn't talk about it. I was wrapped in isolation and prone to heavy drinking because of my Vietnam experience; there was no one I could or would talk to. Certainly not my wife or other family members. I sought help from the nearby Palo Alto VA hospital in 1970 which was dismal at best. After about nine months on a waiting list, I got into a clinic and saw a psychiatrist. The encounter was a rapid-fire staccato of questions and statements from the doctor. He left a prescription for tranquilizers and walked out of the room. The VA at that time had no peer groups, counseling, etc. They were, however, liberal with medications. PTSD had not yet been defined, and vet support groups did not exist. The "community" still used terms like combat stress or maybe even battle fatigue to describe the disorder. Patients who were mentally hurting from PTSD, and other complications were ignored from my own observation and experiences.

My wife got me back in church, as I had left religion when I was about 15 years old. The decision to return to God and the church was a long road for me, but I have remained on that path to this day. I had a lot of pain and mental trash I needed to dump, and I found God had strong shoulders and huge trash bins to leave my hurt and other garbage. Truly a place to give it all up. My wife's gentle nudging, support, and love, I believe, saved my life. I found new friends and fellow vets I could relate to. The sense of community I found in church has been very important for me and helps keep my life in balance. I volunteer in church, community activities, and have become more involved in developing veterans' outreach in our parish to better serve the community.

Those of us who have experienced the horrors of combat have a shared commonality. Those horrible experiences have defined us and where we are today in our lives. Those bad things have long since happened. We can't change them, but how we handle it is our choice. The outcome can be controlled. I have some lessons I learned in my journey these past fifty years:

- People really do care. They will listen, more so now than 50 years ago.
- Find a community of trust for support, and
- Seek help if you're hurting. You don't have to hurt.

I had never participated in a vet's peer group since returning 50 years ago. I recently joined a local group at the VA clinic in Tomball and have been pleasantly surprised with the compassion, care, and brotherhood we feel for one another. This group association I strongly believe is so important to recovery. Do it!

Delta 56 out!

Understanding and Coping with My Mental Challenges

Jesus I. Olivo

My PTSD stems from an incident that occurred in which I was held against my will. It has affected me in many different ways. Without warning, I have episodes of panic attacks, anxiety, and flashbacks where I feel that I'm threatened and in danger.

During these episodes, I can vividly see where I am and who is threatening me. I feel it's occurring in real life, but it's all in my mind. The same scenario plays where I'm going to be captured and I can feel that my life is in danger. I experience different symptoms every time this happens—the hair on the back of my neck stands up, I feel scared and it's hard to breathe, I sweat, my hands shake, and I feel a sense of desperation to secure my loved ones and those around me so that nothing happens to them. My reality is distorted, and I quickly turn into combat mode. I feel the enemy getting closer, wishing to do me harm. This occurs at different times and with different encounters. Sometimes it can be the smell of a cigar. Sometimes it's a certain way the air swirls around me, and sometimes it could be the time of day that triggers the episodes. One thing is for sure: I can hear my heartbeat getting faster and faster and the desperation within me stronger and stronger.

To bring me out of this, sometimes my wife will come to me and tell me that nothing is there. I close my eyes and focus on her voice and what she's saying to make it go away. Her voice is calming and soothing, which makes me feel safe again. After my episode is over, I feel extremely tired and confused; I've lost track of time, and I've lost my bearing. Other times, when I am alone and I'm confused during my episode, I feel that I have to get myself out of it. In order to distract my mind, I have actually hurt myself, such as hitting my hands with something hard. I run into a wall, or in my latest episode, I put my hands on a hot barbecue pit so that the pain would release me.

I realize that I have problem. I realized that before I left the Marine Corps. But I chose not to disclose it to anyone. I tried for a very long time to fix it myself—I drank, I worked, I kept myself busy all the time. I thought all this would keep the memories from creeping back into my mind. Just when I thought I was free and clear, everything would come back again and show me I failed, and I was back to the drawing board. This made me angrier and frustrated. At times, I would explode and break everything in sight. It wasn't until I realized I was broken that I started to accept there was nothing I could do about this. At times, I felt helpless to control it, and I still do. However, I am making progress. Listening to other veterans with experiences like mine and hearing how they cope with those experiences have given me different tools and avenues to follow.

I don't believe that medication will change it, but I do believe I have the power to fix it not only for my sake but for those I love such as my wife and children. Most of all, I need to change for myself. I need to feel like a normal person again and try to recapture my life before I was in the Marine Corps. My peer support group has been one of the greatest sources of healing that I've had in dealing with this problem. It has given me much better tools to begin to understand and cope with my mental challenges.

My PTSD Story

Ross R. Read, MBA

On April 17, 1990, my mentor was killed in the line of duty because he was trying to be nice to a 67-year-old man. I arrived on the scene approximately 45 seconds after Russell was shot twice in the chest at point blank range with his own weapon. Russell was transporting this man to the state mental hospital from the local county hospital. When Russell handcuffed him, he began to sob. Breaking policy, Russell moved the handcuffs from his back to the front of the man he was transporting because—and I can only surmise from my knowledge of how Russell treated people—he felt sorry for him. Russell was repaid for his act of kindness. When Russell went to open the exit door, the patient took Russell's .357 Magnum from his holster, shot him twice in the chest, then walked out the door with Russell's weapon. Russell was supposed to attend my daughter's birthday party a few days later. Instead he spent his last few seconds trying to tell me what I already knew he would say: "Don't take this home."

Russell served three tours in Vietnam. Not a scratch. He became my mentor in 1987 when I graduated from the Marine Corps Military Police Academy. We became close as he took a snotty-nosed kid (I was 19) under his wing and taught him how to be a good cop. I still think about him every day after all these years. The main thing I remember was the first and last lesson he taught me. On day 1 in May 1987, during swing shift patrol, he said, "Whatever you do, however you do it, *never* take the "*shit*" home. Only the things that make you laugh out loud." He meant never take things I would see people do to one another home. At the time, I did not have any idea why that one piece of wisdom was so important.

I went on to spend most of my adult life in the Marine Corps then in civilian law enforcement. I've buried far too many friends, done things to strangers I never thought I would be able to in the line of duty, and informed far too many loved ones that someone they loved would never feel the touch of their face again.

For a long time, those first lessons that Russell passed on to me served me well. As long as I was busy doing what I loved, I could joke with my colleagues while we used a snow shovel to clean up human remains after a shooting or a 3-car pileup, wash my hands, have a cup of coffee, then get back out, and go to work. Over the years, I developed a rather twisted sense of humor. This served me well in dealing with the things I saw. I'm not saying it's nice or even good. It is simply one of my coping mechanisms. I also played golf and spent countless hours behind my drum kit, "transferring the stress to the neighbors," as I called it.

On April 28, 2008, I was injured in the line of duty. Not the first time by far, but it would be the last. After two years of surgeries, painful rehabilitation, rinse, repeat, etc., I was medically retired in May 2010. But the surgeries and, more importantly, the pain would not end there. I have had to endure 17 surgeries on my lower back and 26 to my left leg. There is now more metal in me than there is in any one of the sidearms I carried. I still live with pain that most would not be able to tolerate.

Since the state medically retired me, I have tried to take up my time doing other things. I returned to school and earned my MBA. I went to work as a stockbroker, and I volunteered my time playing drums for several churches and charitable events. Unfortunately, I had to slow down due to the surgeries I had up to this point and the surgeries that were still to come.

I made some significant life changes at the behest of my surgeons and removed or drastically reduced the time I spent doing anything that stressed my system. These changes made it impossible not to have a lot of time to think, ponder, and reflect on my career. This turned out not to be a positive thing. I ended up concentrating on the few painful memories of incidents instead of all the good I had done. I began asking myself the impossible questions: "Could I have prevented this?" "Could I have changed how that came out?" "Why wasn't I able to get there sooner?"

From mid-2010 to early 2014, I began to get worse. It seemed like each week, pain and discomfort went up a little bit more. Whenever I had another surgery, I would then have more time on my hands during recovery. When I tried doing things that took my mind off the things that were bothering me, I would lengthen my recovery time. It was a vicious cycle. My wife noticed that I became more and more introverted and reclusive. This was not me, not the man she married. She did not know why other than I was on massive amounts of opioids from the surgeries and lingering pain. There were several months where we slept in separate bedrooms, as I would wake up fighting.

Things came to a head one afternoon in 2014 at one of my doctors' office. They gave me an injection in my back. For some reason, this injection triggered a memory or feeling in me that completely immobilized me. The doctor called my wife to come and get me, as they were confused about why I went from a 6-foot, 2, 220-pound tough cop to a ball of blubbering goo in the exam room in minutes. It was this event that would change how I fought the demons who had been following me, waiting to pounce.

I started with the Veteran's Administration. They have a PTSD treatment program that helped a little. They also put me on some nasty antidepressants like Zoloft (in addition to the oxycodone and fentanyl I was on already). At one point, I sank as low as you can get. I have talked several people out of hurting themselves in my career. After each encounter, I would tell myself I was successful because they didn't really *want* to hurt themselves. They just wanted some attention. I could not have been more wrong. I won't describe what I did. I will only say I'm lucky and grateful it did not work. No one interceded in my attempt. It simply wasn't my time. I know now I was not done helping others.   I went through the PTSD treatment programs at the VA, and I even got into a medical marijuana study sponsored by the FDA and the VA. While these two programs helped me to an extent, I must credit my current success to talking. That's right. *Talking*. A friend I found through the Veterans of Foreign Wars lost most of his face to a grenade in Vietnam. He wears a prosthesis instead of having a nose and 2 eyes. He took time from his day to talk with me. We just sat and talked about the things we could never tell our wives. Not because we were ashamed, but because we knew our wives would not be able to look at us in the same way again. Not because we were wrong, but because they had no idea of what we were capable.

I fought through depression for several years. I still fight every day. I know that I will never be free of the thoughts and memories I have. I have, however, learned to deal with them in a much more positive way. I *talk* to others. I have been able to get rid of all the opioids, medical marijuana, and even the hardcore antidepressants. It took a few years and hard work, but I now take a mild antidepressant daily and some other nonpsychotropic medications for severe arthritis, but that's all. I live with the physical pain because I don't want to be where I once was.

What I do more than anything else is take time to talk with others who are suffering as I did. I let them know what I have discovered over my journey. I have discovered that we who suffer from PTS have one undeniable thing in common: we all care deeply about our fellow human beings. Because of this, I submit: If we did not have the ability to love and have empathy for our fellow human beings, the things we have seen and done would not have such a profound effect upon us. While that is my theory, I have found it to be true in each of the military, law enforcement, firefighters, nurses, and other first responders I have counseled. I know there will never be a cure for PTS. (I leave out the *D* as I don't see it as a disorder. You can't catch it. You cannot pass it on. PTS is an injury suffered by the people who are on the front lines every day.) There is no cure. We can treat PTS and live normal lives while doing so.

Just talk! Talk to someone who has been where you are. They can help you pull yourself from the hole you believe you have dug. They can help you look forward to days with hope and nights without terror. Believe it or not, you are helping them more than they are helping you. That's how it works for me anyway. The more I can help other people with PTS, the less help I need with my own.

Personal Health and Well-Being

Introduction

The road to better health rests within you. The first step is to know what you want from your health and why. Knowing your health goals may not be a simple task, yet it is an important step toward reaching your full potential. The following tool invites you to think about where you are now with your health and well-being and where you want to be in the future. It begins by exploring your vision for living life fully and being as healthy as you can be.

Health and You as a Whole Person

People often only think of going to the doctor when they are sick, need a routine checkup, or have a medical condition. Living life fully and optimizing health and well-being go beyond just not being sick. It means understanding what matters to you and looking at all aspects in life that contribute to a sense of well-being. This tool will help you explore all areas of your life so your health care team can help you plan not just for your medical needs but for your "life" needs.

The Components of Health and Well-Being

> You + Self Care + Professional Care = Health Care

The components of health and well-being is a picture to help you think about your whole health. All the areas in the box are important and connected. Improving one area can benefit other areas in your life and influence your overall physical, emotional, and mental health and well-being. The human body and mind have tremendous capacity to heal, and these innate healing abilities are strengthened or weakened by many factors that we can influence. The innermost circle represents you, your values, and what really matters to you. The next circle is your self-care, the circumstances, and choices you make in your day-to-day life. The outer ring represents professional care, such as medical care, tests, medications, surgery, counseling, and complementary approaches, such as acupuncture and mind-body therapies.

You

You are the expert of your life, values, goals, and priorities. Only you can know *why* you want your health. Only you can know what really matters to you. And this needs to be the driver of your health and your health care. You are the most important person, the captain of the team, when it comes to making choices that influence your health and well-being. You are the captain of your team, and your medical team are some of the invited players.

Mindful Awareness

Mindfulness is simply being fully aware or paying attention. Sometimes, we go through our daily lives on autopilot and aren't fully present in the here and now. We often dwell on the past and plan out events in the future. We don't spend much time really noticing what is happening right now. We just pay attention and notice without judging or trying to fix it. Your body and mind send you signals constantly, but if your attention is elsewhere, you don't notice. Then the signals that began as whispers become screams. For example, when you miss the whispers of an early discomfort or a sad feeling, you miss the opportunity to react until it grows into real pain or depression. Being mindful, or aware, allows you to make conscious, proactive choices about every aspect of your health. Mindfulness connects you to each component of your well-being and to your whole self.

The Areas of Self-Care

Working your body "energy and flexibility"

Movement and exercise increase your energy and flexibility and affects the state of your body, your mind, and emotions. Studies show that regular exercise reduces risk factors by lowering blood pressure and cholesterol, two major contributors to the number one killer, heart disease. Physical activities of all kinds are beneficial and increase strength, flexibility, endurance, and balance. Finding what you enjoy and what works for you is important and may include activities like walking, dancing, gardening, swimming, bicycling, lifting weights, or working out in a gym.

Recharge "rest and sleep"

Rest, relaxation, and sleep recharge and refuel you. Sleep is critical for important bodily and mind functions. Rest, relaxation, and leisure activities create a sense of peace and calm and lower stress. You may also find that doing physical activities, spending time with family and friends, spending time in nature, completing a significant challenge, or working on a hobby helps you to recharge. Paying attention to the balance between activity and rest is important for optimal health.

Food and drink "nourishing and fueling"

What you eat and drink can nourish and strengthen your body and mind. Your decisions about what you eat and drink impact your mood, energy level, and physical health and performance. Developing healthy drinking and eating habits that fit your lifestyle, taking supplements that support your health goals, and limiting substances like alcohol, caffeine, and nicotine keep your body properly fueled.

Personal development "personal life and work life"

No matter what stage you are at in life, addressing your personal or work life is hugely important. This means taking a look at how you spend your time and energy throughout the day and whether those activities fuel you or drain you. Does the balance of where and how you spend your energy line up with what matters to you? How do you feel about your finances, and how are they impacting your life? These factors affect not only your happiness but also your health.

Family, friends, and coworkers "hearing and being heard"

Your social relationships and whether you feel isolated or connected to others are associated with whether or not you get sick, stay sick, and even how likely you are to die prematurely. In good times and challenging times, it helps to have caring and supportive relationships with people with whom you can talk to openly and know that they really listen to you. You have a natural communication style, as do the people around you. You can learn different ways to improve your communication skills and strengthen relationships. You can also choose to spend more time with your healthy relationships and limit those that are draining or negative.

Spirit and soul "growing and connecting"

A sense of meaning and purpose in life and a connection to things outside of you are words that describe the core of what is really important to many people. Where do you turn for a sense of strength and comfort in difficult times? Some people turn to faith, religious practice, or time in nature. Some connect with art or music or prefer quiet time alone. You may express this as a guiding principle for living and giving, a regard for others, or a connection with your inner self in ways that fuel you.

Surroundings "physical and emotional"

The environment where you spend time a lot of time (like at home or work), both inside and outdoors, directly affects you and your health. You may have issues with basic needs, such as safety or things like clutter, noise, smells, chemicals, poor lighting, or water quality that keep you from being your best. Some of these factors, you may be able to impact or change and some you may not. It all begins with paying attention to the influences of your environment on your life and your health and improving what you can. It matters to have safe, comfortable, and healthy spaces.

Power of the mind "strengthen and listen"

The mind directly impacts the state of your body in both positive and negative ways. Think of a lemon and you salivate. Think of something that stresses you and your heart rate and blood pressure jump. Learning to use this connection intentionally for positive effects is easy to do. Mind-body practices strengthen the communication between your body, brain, and mind. Think about highly trained athletes or warriors who use the power of their mind to visualize success or people who use the power of their mind to lower their blood pressure or control pain. You can learn to optimize your body's ability to heal and cope better with mental and physical stress by using mind-body techniques.

Professional care "engaged and proactive"

The components of health and well-being represent your relationship with your health care team and others who are a part of your team. This includes preventive care (including immunizations, weight control, and not smoking) and early detection of disease (such as blood pressure readings and cancer screenings like Pap smears and colonoscopies). It also includes being evaluated for signs or symptoms of problems and often results in tests and diagnostics, followed by interventions or treatments for the full range of conditions or diseases. Drawing on the best and most effective treatments or approaches is critical and includes traditional or conventional services (such as medications, counseling, and surgery) as well as complementary approaches (like acupuncture, supplements, and mind-body therapies). The plan to manage or treat diseases, as well as preventing diseases, will all include strategies that are rooted in your self-care.

(Source: Handout from VHA and the Office of Patient-Centered Care and Cultural Transformation)

Reach Out to be Heard

Robert Garcia

My story begins in 1977 when I was three years old. People often have fond memories of their childhood. Unfortunately I did not. My first memory was seeing my dad hitting my mom. The last straw was when my dad tried to hit me. That's when we moved out and went to live with my grandmother.

At five years old, I was getting beat up all the time by the same guy. One day, I fought back, and that's when I learned that violence was the answer. This continued for the next thirty years of my life. By the time I was nine years old, I had already started drinking, tried marijuana, smoked cigarettes, broke into a house, watched pornography, carried a pistol at times, ran from the cops, and got to drive my grandmother's truck around. At thirteen, I was already sexually active and went to my first strip club and would drive from Texas to Louisiana.

I lived a life of violence, believing that was the answer. I started selling drugs in high school, and throughout school I didn't really care much. I never thought I'd make it past eighteen, so why worry about a formal education? Then Desert Storm happened. My life was going nowhere, and even though I have always been bad, I've always been proud to be an American.

I walked into the first recruiter's door and said, "Where do I sign?" They asked why I was so gung ho, in which my response was "Y'all going to let me kill people, right?" which led them to say, "Son, you're in the wrong branch. The Marines are next door." So I walked next door, opened the door, and asked,

"Are y'all going to let me kill somebody?" Their response was "Come sign right here!"

I took the ASVAB and passed. The only problem with that was I didn't graduate high school, and I thought if I got my GED, then I would go. In May of 1994, I was arrested and convicted of aggravated assault with a deadly weapon with intent to kill. I got my GED and tried to join the military again, but they wouldn't take a convicted felon. Later, I learned that they would make an exception for felonies on a case by case basis, so I tried again only to find out I had, by this time, too many tattoos. Three strikes and I was out.

After the disappointment of not being able to enlist, I gave up all hope of having a good life and went full force to the only life I knew. Violence solved my problems. From being shot at, stabbed, hit in fistfights, you name it, I was in it. I assumed I would never make it to 21. My mentality was that if I couldn't accept two facts—one, I could die today, and two, I could go to prison for the rest of my life—then I wouldn't leave the house.

After I turned 21, I decided to just live my life day-to-day only expecting to die. I found myself in and out of trouble with authorities, fighting everywhere I went. I fought anyone I could. I was fighting in my own house, and most of those battles were about me fighting my own thoughts in my own head.

At 32, I broke into a vacant house with a bottle of alcohol and a pistol to commit suicide, yelling out to God that He is not real because if He were, then how could He allow everything I saw to happen? With the pistol to my head and my finger on the trigger, as I began to squeeze, God showed up. I fell to my knees with my arms raised up in full surrender to Him. For the next three years, I was still fighting, drinking, and other things, but something was different. I started having a conscience. When I did wrong, I would worry if the people I hurt would be okay. At 35, I met a man who showed me what being a real brother in Christ was all about. We read the Bible and prayed together. I joined a church and was baptized.

2010 was the last time I drank alcohol, smoked cigarettes, and used violence to solve problems. I'm not saying that I don't struggle with it, but I'm saying that I've learned a different way to solve problems. It's only through Jesus Christ. I always thought that I was created for bad and to fight, but that's only half right. I'm created to fight, that is, "fight the good fight of faith" (1 Timothy 6:12).

In 2012, I surrendered to full-time ministry. God gave me the name "Luke 2:49 Ministries—About my Father's Business." It has taken me to prisons, the streets, shelters, halfway homes, churches, and even other continents to bring hope to the hopeless and love for those who know not love. I don't know how my story ends, but I do know I have an eternity promised to me and a freedom only given through my relationship with Jesus Christ. I still have my moments, almost daily, but it's my faith in Jesus that keeps me going, knowing how loving He is to love a sinner like me. In the same aspect, if He can forgive me, I know He can forgive you. The Bible says in Romans 10:10, "For with the heart a person believes, resulting in righteousness, and with the mouth he confesses, resulting in salvation." My prayer today is that if you find yourself feeling hopeless, may you find hope in our Lord and Savior Jesus Christ. Not only can he set you free but he can give you a new life.

In closing, no one has ever fought a war by himself. We all need backup and people who are there for us to speak truth into our life. I would encourage you to not remain silent but to reach out to be heard so you can get the help you need.

Propelled for Purpose

Hannah Clark

At the age of 12—an *almost* teenage girl where my transition of self-development and becoming was manifesting—I suddenly embraced the reality of abandonment. My father unexpectedly walked out on our family after 19 years of marriage to my mother. In a short period of time, my parents divorced, my maternal grandfather passed due to pancreatic cancer, and my brother had given up his baseball career to drugs. I felt that I had lost complete control of my life, oblivious to the fact that I was never the one in control to begin with. Because I had unnoticeably welcomed abandonment into my life, all I would seek for years to come was the love and acceptance of others, which would eventually lead to the formation of my eating disorder, not knowing that this very moment would pave the way in developing the woman I acknowledge, love, and accept today.

For years, I lived in a constant state of depression, fear, anxiety, and denial while occasionally combating the thoughts of suicide. From the time I graduated high school, I was looking to fill the void through the validation of people, which led me into a toxic relationship and eventually a marriage with a man whom I barely knew. After a few short months, I found out that I was expecting. Due to my upbringing, personal morals, and the pressure of others, I knew that I did not want to welcome an unborn child into the world out of wedlock. This added much more pressure, as I was not only fighting a secret battle for my life but now the precious life inside my womb. At 5 months of being pregnant, I was weighing roughly 87 pounds and found myself starting to physically shut down. I knew if I weren't going to fight for myself, then I would fight for the life forming inside me, which inspired me to publicly seek help and begin treatment for the next 4 months at one of the largest eating disorder facilities in the nation.

Shortly after meeting the requirements to graduate from the program, I welcomed my beautiful and healthy 8-pound, 11-ounce baby girl into the world, who still, to this day, serves as a living representation of the miracles of our Lord and Savior. Two weeks after my daughter was born, my husband at the time and I were separated due to ongoing issues. A couple of weeks later, I tried to rekindle things for the sake of my newborn. I was officially living in misery while fighting the weight of my battles. Because I did not want to appear as a failure by others, I decided to "stick it out" in hopes of making things work. Fifteen short months later, I found out that I was expecting child number two. I now felt trapped, and the small flame I saw at the end of the tunnel was suddenly burned out. My depression progressed, and I now felt abandoned by God. Time went on, and I had my precious little boy that is my daily reminder of the promises of God. As I sought godly counsel and an ample amount of time in prayer, I decided that it was time for a change for my babies and myself and eventually divorced at the age of 21, starting over with nothing more than a dedicated heart and willing spirit.

Though the last several years have been a journey of surrendering and healing, the Lord has showed Himself faithful time after time, revealing Himself as only He can. It wasn't until I began to accept the beauty in my scars and the wisdom in my wounds that I still possessed the potential for a beautiful tomorrow. Realizing the importance of this truth, I openly forgave myself, thanked those who helped write my story amid the pain, and shut the door to my past. This is when the overflow of opportunity and new creativity were brought to light. Following my journey of healing, I have since remarried my Prince Charming—my purpose mate and love of my life—whom I didn't believe existed and received a third bonus child whom I love, admire, and adore. Though my story remains to unfold, it is my utmost joy to serve as a living testament and vessel in the kingdom alongside my husband, Joshua, and our three precious children. I pray that your testimony will be used as a weapon to break curses from your bloodline and that you will continue to exceed every expectation that this world has with only the power and determination that you possess. May you surrender to the healing within and allow your story to be a platform that you stand on rather than a prison that you live in. I am praying for you in light and love.

*****

Hannah Clark Biography

Meet Hannah Clark. As a certified life coach, inspirational speaker, philanthropist, PTSD and MST counselor, chaplain, wife, mother of three, businesswoman, and mental health advocate, Hannah Clark is solely devoted to enriching, ennobling, and empowering the lives of others by portraying a lifestyle of women empowerment. With one goal in mind, Hannah passionately pursues and promotes the overall well-being and success to all facets around *the* country. As a strong woman of faith, Hannah shares her story with a positive and inimitable transparency that allows *all walks of life* to gravitate to her tender spirit.

How Forgiveness and Gratitude Transformed My Life

Jo Ann Rotermund

As a child, I was taught that I must never, never ever get angry at anyone and then express my anger. Whenever I would come home from school or from playing outside with other children and tell my mother how very upset I was about something that had been said to me, like a teasing I had endured or being made wrong for being a preacher's kid or for being fat, my mother would say, "Just put a smile on your face and go on. Don't let it bother you." So I learned to stuff all my upsets, put a smile on my face, and go on about my life. As a teenager, I was often complimented for my beautiful smile, so of course, I kept smiling no matter what happened or what was said to me.

I even got married and had two children while still stuffing all my upsets and keeping a smile on my face. I would get upset and have it out with my husband about once a year or less. Finally, during my eighth year of marriage, some things began to change. I sank into a deep depression and spent about 9 months in bed just existing with my baby daughter beside me before I began to realize something was very wrong and I needed help.

About that time, the speaker for a PTA meeting at my daughter's school was an emotional therapist. I heard her speak, liked her very much, and promptly started going to her for help with my deep depression.

She helped me change my life in many wonderful ways and opened my mind to many new ways of thinking and living. I loved what I was learning and opening up to so much that I was constantly asking her for more except in one particular area. No matter what she did or said or tried, she could not get me to express any anger. She tried for many months in many different ways. But I was simply incapable of doing it. She finally gave up and told me I was by far the most passive person she had ever met.

Nevertheless, I was so happy with all that I was learning that I continued seeing her until we moved 2000 miles away for my husband's work. And I did not seek out another therapist. What I did was jump into my new life and my new world with excitement and joy, remembering all that I had learned from my therapy. We were all very happy with our new home and our new lives in upstate New York. Life was good!

A few months after we were there, a gasoline crisis happened and the lines at gas stations were long and slow, requiring a lot of patience to get gas. Once I finally got to the pumps, my tank was sitting on empty, and I chose to fill it, which took a while. Finally, the man behind me in line got angry and started yelling at me. I yelled back then turned my back to him and never looked his way again.

Thinking about it at home, I realized I had actually gotten angry and yelled back at that guy. Wow! OMG! I was very pleased with myself. Although I didn't do it, I wanted to run to the phone and call my therapist to tell her about it. Two or three weeks later, something happened while I was out running errands and shopping, and once again someone angrily yelled at me. Once again, I yelled back. OMG!

Again, thinking about it later at home, I was very, very pleased and happy with myself. *Wow!* I actually got angry and yelled at a total stranger! OMG! OMG! OMG! Finally I was allowing myself to get angry and express it. And it actually felt really, really good. Amazingly good! No wonder my parents didn't want me to express anger. It was almost as good as having sex! And no wonder my therapist worked so hard to get me to express some anger. *Wow!*

From that point on, I expressed anger more and more and more often at home, around friends, on the phone, or out in public with total strangers. It felt *good*! Out in public, I always wanted to be sure that many people as possible would hear me screaming about how right I was and how wrong the other person was. The better it felt, the more anger I expressed to anyone, anywhere, anytime. I was very, very proud of myself. I was finally doing what my therapist had tried so hard to get me to do… I thought.

However, since I had never expressed any anger around my therapist, we never discussed how to deal with anger when I felt it and especially when I expressed it. I actually believed that getting angry and fully expressing it was really a good thing. It felt so good, and I was so sure of myself that I did not seek out another therapist for coaching of any sort. I am sure you can guess what happened. Yes, I lost all control of my anger.

When we went shopping, my teenage daughters would beg me, "Please, please promise us you won't scream at anyone in the mall or the store." I always promised not to scream, and I would always scream anyway. Of course, my daughters and my husband were very unhappy with my screaming in public. However, they did not know how to get me to stop any more than I knew how to stop myself. I just couldn't do it. We all learned to just accept it and life went on.

Eventually God took charge by regularly putting books, magazine articles, and TV programs about forgiveness in front of me. And eventually, I started studying forgiveness. I read everything I could find on forgiveness, and I went to numerous workshops. I forgave, forgave, and forgave everyone for everything, starting as far back as age four. I had so much rage stuffed within me. It took a lot of forgiving over several years to clear it all out. But it was definitely worth it. So totally and completely worth it!

My life changed radically as a result of my willingness to forgive everyone for every unhappy thing that had ever happened in my life. In the process, I also learned to forgive myself, and that made a tremendous difference as well.

Additionally, in the process of studying about forgiveness, I learned to express gratitude many times a day every single day. Expressing gratitude, especially making a written list of 20 or more people, places, things you are grateful for makes forgiveness much, much easier. It also will take away your anger if you find yourself in a situation where you are upset about something, but you need to be happy and joyful right now. Expressing gratitude is one of the most powerful positive habits you can develop.

Eventually, I wanted everyone to know the incredible freedom, inner power, and joy I had found through gratitude and forgiveness. I eventually started speaking and teaching forgiveness, and later, I wrote a book.

My husband is 84, and I am 76. We have been married for 52 years. We are very happy together. I know with absolute certainty that could not have happened without forgiveness in our lives. I wish tremendous gratitude and total forgiveness for you in your life.

> Faith is to believe what you do not see; the reward of this faith is to see what you believe.
>
> --- SAINT AUGUSTINE ---

The Trauma of Losing a Child

J. Bennett

Coming home (7 days after the accident)

Missing a piece of my heart. That is the only way to describe the pain after losing a child. It is an empty feeling, a feeling deep in your chest. It is difficult to breathe and to take a deep breath. Still, three years later, I find myself struggling to take a full, deep breath. Coming home from the hospital without my son was excruciating. I never knew a pain like this existed.

I lay on the floor of his bedroom, smelled his dirty clothes, and hugged his favorite stuffed animal. He was only 18 months old. This wasn't supposed to happen. He should have grown old. I was supposed to go first.

Those first few days at home were the most difficult. I didn't want to live anymore. I would lie in bed and cry, a wailing cry I didn't know I was capable of. I told my husband, "I just want to die." I wasn't sure how I could go on. Jackson was my perfect little boy, my only son, and now he was gone. Suddenly gone. And it was my fault.

Before

Have you ever had a moment that you thought to yourself, *Wow, this is it! It doesn't get better than this.* It seems like it was only a few hours before my son's accident that I thought to myself, *This is the happiest I have ever been.* I looked down at my son as he sang "Row, row, row your boat" and told myself, "Remember this feeling." I felt so blessed to have this beautiful, smart, healthy little boy. He was so happy. Everyone who met him instantly fell in love. He had never met a stranger; he treated everyone like family. Little did I know, I was about to lose him.

Jackson James was born 2 days before Christmas. He was our third child, and we thought he was going to be our last. After having two girls, my husband and I were so excited to have a little boy in the house. Football, basketball, trucks, trains, playing in dirt—we were looking forward to it all. And Jackson was just that. He was all boy. Rough and tumble but also so sweet and full of life. It was a known fact that Jackson gave the best hugs. He was also a very determined child. He reached all his developmental milestones early. I truly thought he was destined for greatness. There was something so special about him.

We live in the suburbs of Houston, Texas. We have a pool in our backyard, and we spent most summer days swimming. The summers are so hot, and being in the pool was the best way for the kids to play outside. We wanted our youngest child to have fun with us in the pool too. After he turned 1 year, we enrolled him in swimming lessons at a local recreation center. Since he was under 3 years of age, he was in parent-child swim lessons group. My husband and I took turns taking him to lessons. Jackson loved playing in the water. We sang songs, played games in the water, and worked on kicking and moving his arms. We even encouraged him to jump into the water to us. He was fearless, and we loved it. We were so proud of our water baby. These lessons made him very comfortable in the water. After the completion of the lessons, I asked the instructor if there was anything else we could do at this age to work with him on swimming. She said that he had learned everything he could at this age. I was unaware of any other swim programs—such as survival swimming—that he could take. So we decided that we would work with him at home.

We take safety in our home very seriously. I work as an emergency room nurse and have seen many incidents of children who fall or are involved in car accidents. Occasionally I have seen children come in after a choking incident, electrical shock, and SIDS, possibly related to co-sleeping. From my experiences, we took precautions we felt were keeping him safe: we put gates on the stairs, kept him rear facing in his car seat, put electrical outlet covers, cut his food into small bites, and practice safe sleep habits. I wouldn't even let him climb on a playground without following him. As for the pool, I naively thought if he could not get past our back door, he would be safe. We are good parents who watch our children. We never took our eyes off him when he was in the pool. He was either in our arms or in a puddle jumper floatation device.

The Accident

One summer day, we were out of routine. We were down to one car and my husband needed a way to get to work. It was my day off. My husband and I worked opposite each other, so either I or he would be home with the kids. I had a choice. I could either let my husband use the van and be without a car all day, or I could drive him to and from work. Since I had a few things I wanted to do, I decided I would take him to work.

After I fed the kids dinner, I made a plate for my husband to reheat when he got home. He usually gets off work at 8 p.m. on Saturday, but since it was close to Jackson's bedtime, he made arrangements that we could pick him up at 7 p.m. instead. That way, we wouldn't be dealing with a grumpy toddler at the end of the day. I started packing up the kids to load them into the car. I cleaned Jackson's face from dinner, put on his shoes, grabbed his diaper bag, and placed him on my hip. The girls made their way to the van.

It was at that point I realized I needed to let the dogs outside. I didn't want them to have an accident in the house. We were going to be gone for about an hour. I ran over to the back door, with Jackson still on my hip, and I made the decision to unlock the dog door. We only used the dog door when we were going to be away from the house for long period of times because we knew it was a risk for our toddler. But this evening, we were ready to leave, and I was too impatient to wait for them to go potty and let them back inside. I unlocked the dead bolt, opened the heavy glass door, and took the cover off the dog door that was on our storm door. I set the cover to the side of the wall, and I remember looking at it, thinking to myself, *Remember you did this.* Then we left.

When we returned, I remember walking into the house as a family. My husband went to reheat his dinner. We had a few minutes before I was going to start the bedtime routine, so I asked my husband if I could have a 5-minute break in our room, just a few minutes of peace alone. I asked him, "Will you watch Jackson?" I never left a room without making sure someone had their eyes on him. I went into my room and lay on my bed.

After a few minutes, I peeked my head outside my bedroom door, and I saw my husband sitting on the couch eating his dinner in front of the TV. I guess I assumed Jackson would be sitting right next to him, but he wasn't there. I asked him, "Where is Jackson?" He replied, "He is upstairs playing with the girls." This was a normal occurrence. We have a large game room at the top of the stairs. Everything is safe, and his older sister, who was 10 at the time, was great with him. I went back into the room. I left my door open. I could hear the girls, but I couldn't hear Jackson. I had a horrible, uneasy feeling, a feeling that I needed to find Jackson now. I went back to the living room and asked my husband again, "Where is Jackson?" He called out, "Girls, is Jackson up there with you?" They shouted back, "No."

That is when I realized I forgot to relock the dog door. I ran as fast as I could out the back door and found my son lying facedown in the pool. He was still wearing his red "I'm on Team Dad" shirt and khaki shorts. He wasn't supposed to be swimming. We thought he was safe inside our home. Come to find out, this is how most toddlers drown.

I jumped into the pool and pulled him out to the side. His skin was warm and pink. It had only been a few minutes. Maybe he just fell in? I yelled out for my husband, but he was already there. I yelled, "Call 911!" I begged Jackson to wake up, but I quickly realized he was gone. I started rescue breaths and chest compressions as we waited on the ambulance. I had done CPR on people many times but never a child. It was the most difficult thing I have ever had to do.

The paramedics arrived and intubated him, and he regained a heartbeat. He was then transported to my emergency room, my second home, my work family. Surrounded by my coworkers and friends, he was stabilized and flown to a children's hospital for further care. Four days later, he was declared brain-dead. Three days after that, we said our last goodbye as he was wheeled to the operating suite to donate his organs.

After

Experiencing a sudden and traumatic loss changed me. My needs changed. My priorities changed. Things I used to think were important no longer mattered. I experienced such a deep, emotional pain that I almost wished there was something physically wrong with me to help explain it. As an emergency room nurse, I take care of patients who are suicidal and depressed. Some of these patients cut themselves. I never understood why someone would do that. I guess I ignorantly thought that they were seeking attention. But after having this experience, I gained an understanding of why someone would do that. It's so as to have a physical source of pain. To have an outlet for their pain.

For me, this was not an option. I had to stay strong for my family. They needed me now more than ever. I didn't want them to experience any more loss. Yes, they saw me cry, but we never stopped talking about Jackson. He was still everywhere inside our home. At times, I found it difficult to be a support person for my husband. If I was having a good day, it took a lot of emotional energy for me to help him when he was having a bad day. We would talk about Jackson, watch home videos, and look at pictures together, remembering all the wonderful times we had together.

I sought counseling, but I quickly discovered it wasn't for me. Having to explain the situation and how I was feeling to a stranger felt so strange to me. I am very fortunate to have an amazing group of friends who knew Jackson and who loved Jackson themselves. They let me confide in them anytime. It made sense to talk to them. The hard part was knowing when to reach out before the grief became too intense. I did not want to be a burden on my friends, but they also didn't want to me see me hurting. Reaching out to my support system made a world of difference.

Our family was incredibly supportive. My mother stayed with us for about a month after his death and helped us with the day-to-day. My work was also amazing; coworkers donated paid time off so I could recover at home. I feel incredibly blessed to be surrounded by support and love from so many.

Recovery

I found it helped to have plans for the day. The days I didn't have plans, I had a hard time simply getting out of bed. The grief would take over, and I would lie in bed and cry. Plans were always easier made the day before. It helped to have a plan to get out of bed and to be ready to leave the house by a certain time. It helped to stay busy and surround myself with people who wanted to see me well. It felt good to get out of the house and take my daughters somewhere fun. After all, it was their summer vacation and I wanted them to have a good time.

Shortly after we lost Jackson, we welcomed another son. He did not—and never will—replace Jackson, but he surely did help to fill the hole left in our hearts. He has brought us so much life and love in our pain. We thought for sure we were finished having children after we had Jackson. He was not in our original plans, and we are so blessed to have him.

One of the hardest parts, still to this day, is when people ask questions in innocent conversations. A typical question is "How many children do you have?" I have such a hard time answering this question. If I say 4, they usually ask, "How many boys and girls?" and "How old are they?" Sometimes I include Jackson, and it usually involves sharing my loss. This can make people uncomfortable, so I would choose this option carefully. It hurts deep in my heart when I don't include Jackson, but sometimes it is easier that way.

I lost my son to something that could have been prevented. We lost him while he was in the care of both myself and my husband. I used to worry about being judged as a bad and neglectful parent. I judged myself this way even though I knew I was a good parent. I didn't know that drowning is the leading cause of accidental death in children from ages 1–4. I didn't know that most toddlers drown during nonswim times, times when parents think they are safe inside their home. I didn't know about "layers of protection," such as having multiple barriers to prevent your child from reaching the pool, and that relying on a door is just not enough. I didn't know about survival swimming lessons.

It took me about 2 years to gain the strength to begin speaking about Jackson's drowning. I no longer told people I lost my son in an accident. I began telling them that he drowned. I have met many other wonderful parents who have lost their child to drowning in a similar situation. The child wanders off during a lapse in supervision and finds the water. Children are drawn to the water. Why wouldn't they be? Our culture makes being in the water so much fun. We make them feel safe and feel comfortable before they can rescue themselves if they find the water alone.

The stigma surrounding drownings is that parents aren't watching their children. Yes, that is true, but were parents also are not watching when children draw on the wall or put on makeup all over their face? The truth is drowning is fast and it is silent and it will continue to happen until we change the culture and break the stigma surrounding drowning accidents. This is how I decided to help.

I wish someone would have told me the truth about drowning. I wish I had had more education on drowning prevention. I am now an advocate for childhood drowning prevention. I am involved in many organizations, operate a chapter of a 501(c)(3) nonprofit organization, and am a founding member of a national multiorganizational educational project. Within the hospital system I work for, I created a drowning prevention campaign as well as organized a work group within the injury prevention committee at our local regional advisory council for EMS and trauma.

Sharing Jackson's story and educating parents has become a passion of mine. I don't want any other family to experience this preventable loss. I believe a lot needs to be done to protect future generations of children, and I am determined to help make those changes in our culture. I believe that by turning my grief into action, I have become much stronger. It has helped me immensely in my pain. It has given me a greater reason for living.

I know I will never be without pain. I will never be able to take Jackson to his first day of school. I will never see him play in a sport or graduate high school. I won't be able to see him fall in love and create a family of his own. How I wish I could go back in time with the knowledge I now have and prevent his death, but I can't. I can only move forward, share his story, and hope that someone will learn from my mistakes and save their child.

This summer, we had the opportunity to meet the little boy who received Jackson's heart. He was 7 months old at the time of the transplant. He had never left the hospital. His family felt he only had a few more days, and then they received the word of a 99 percent donor match. This little boy is now 3 and a half years old living in Anchorage, Alaska. Meeting this family and listening to my son's heart beating again is one of the best moments of my life. I am grateful to have had this opportunity and excited to watch him grow.

The loss of a child is indeed traumatic. I have chosen to look for the good and find the positive that has come from this horrible event. It did not happen overnight. Don't expect things to simply get better. Plan on a roller coaster of emotions, and know that no one else will truly understand your pain. Confide in those who are close to you. Rely on your support system. Make plans. Make some good happen from your trauma. Help others. Live life to the fullest.

My Beautiful Blue-Eyed Christopher

Sandy Gambill

Christopher was a blue-eyed, blond-haired boy with a sweet smile. He was a soft-spirited little boy who was never in a hurry. I had Christopher when I was in my early 20's, and I was very energetic as a mom.

He was born on July 20, 1985. The birth was difficult, as I was in labor for 25 hours. They finally induced me, but he still was not ready to come into this world. Finally, with the use of forceps, he was forced into the world. I was so happy to meet him, so elated that he had ten fingers and ten toes and a roof in his mouth. He was a sweet little baby boy with a very good temperament. Bathed, changed, and fed, he was a happy baby.

As he grew up, we began to see behaviors we were not familiar with. It was brought to our attention in Montessori school that Christopher would stare into space and that even waving hands in front of his face would not get his attention. We had him tested, and they found nothing wrong. This was the early 90s, an era of ADHD and ADD medications. We had no clue what any of these conditions were. He began school, and everything changed. They gave us an ultimatum: either put Christopher on medication or he could not come back to school. That was pretty brutal for me who had no idea, even after researching, about ADD and ADHD. At age six, Christopher was put on Ritalin after being tested and diagnosed with ADD and ADHD. He became malnourished and lost a lot of weight. Both Christopher and I were so lost. I took him off Ritalin, only for his medication to be changed time and time again by his doctor. He was in counseling and the Big Brother program, as I was a single parent and needed him to have a support system. Difficulty persisted.

When Christopher was nine, I remarried, and things went well for a while. With years of behavioral problems due to meds, at age thirteen, we began to see drastic changes. He began smoking pot, and I found out he was selling his Adderall at school. I took him off of the medication immediately. This was when things began to get worse. He was still in counseling, and we put him in Palmer Drug Abuse Program (PDAP). He was sixteen by this time and out of control, using harder drugs. We started to learn about drug rehabs and checked him into several. The cost added up to $30,000, which we could not afford at the time. By the age of nineteen, he was on heroin. We contacted rehabs and they accepted him, but at this point, he would not go. He was in and out of our home.

In October 2010, I was doing workout boot camps and began to feel bad. I went to the doctor and found out that my aorta was tattered and that I needed open heart surgery in two weeks. I was in shock and so scared. I endured the surgery and worked hard to complete all my physical therapy.

Christopher was now 24 and working for me, as I owned my own company. He seemed to be off the hard drugs by this time. He met an employee of mine, and they ended up getting pregnant and having my beautiful grandson, Christian. Not long after his birth, they both were on heroin. She ended up pregnant again. This time with a little girl they named Hope. The mother was on heroin during her entire pregnancy. Soon after, they both quit working for me, got caught stealing, and went to prison—Christopher for 5 years and she for 6 months. In January 2011, my husband and I got custody of the children.

Christian was one year old, and Hope was twelve weeks old. I was still recovering from open heart surgery.

Challenging times were upon us to say the least. After the mother got out of prison, she was on probation and had to complete a parenting program. She did nothing she was told and ended back on drugs. She gave up her rights to her children and eventually went back to prison. Christopher got cleaned up while he was in prison. I would take his son to go visit him and enjoy our time while he was sober. He was my son again. I cherished that time. He called me one day and told me he was getting out early. He had only spent 10 months in prison. He paroled out to our home and stayed for 1 week, but he was not allowed to be at our home because the children were there. He then moved into a halfway house, which we knew nothing about.

My middle son had become an addict with the help of his brother. The boys are five years apart. At age 14, my middle son detected type 1 diabetes. This was scary, and I always thought I would lose him because of the disease. Upon coming out of prison, Christopher began running around with his brother, who was still on drugs. His brother asked him to go with him to do a drug deal. They had another friend with them as well. As they parked, two men approached the car windows with guns. The guy in the back seat panicked and shot his gun, and they all started to shoot. Christopher was hit in the chest, and it paralyzed him from the chest down. He had been out of prison for 6 weeks and could do 800 push-ups and now paralyzed!

All our lives had changed. He was in the hospital for 3 months and intensive care for 1 month. My middle son was a mess, still using and wanting to die, blaming himself. Christopher finally came home, and it was hectic with babies and a younger 10-year-old son. We had to decide to adopt out our grandchildren. This was the hardest thing I have ever done in my life. It was very hard on Christopher. We were put in a position to pick: take care of the babies or take care of Chris. He could not reside with them. I would go on to take care of Christopher for 3 years. He went through a lot of mental torture. He attended counseling, and we kept him as busy as we could. They gave him way too many drugs upon leaving the hospital. I would have to call a mental health warrant on him due to abuse. He got a bedsore which got so big and infected that he ended up with sepsis in his entire body and brain. He was in Kindred Hospital for 30 days. He did not know anybody.

After that was over, he got clean. Not even a cigarette. He was told that in order to heal, he had to be super healthy. So he did it and got into TIRR Memorial Hermann for PT. He was going 3 days per week and had regained feeling now from his chest to his waist.

These are the times I adored—sitting on the back porch drinking coffee and talking in the mornings. We would laugh and cut up. It was so nice to be able to visit my son sober. He was being healthy, eating good, sleeping well, and going to therapy 3 days per week. He was excited about life again. Then in May, I could see him slipping. First, his granddad died. His little brother, now 13, was also diagnosed with type 1 diabetes.

Chris was very close to his little brother. This was a shock to the entire family. We were all stunned and sad for him. Within 3 weeks, Christopher overdosed. It was all too much. Unless you have been through this, it is unexplainable. I am grateful for our program of Al-Anon. Without our program, I do not believe our family could have remained intact. We all need tools to deal with addiction or mental issues. We are so grateful for the 29 years we had with our son. He is missed and loved and always will be.

*****

Sandy Gambill Biography

Sandy is married and has three sons aged 34, 28, and 18. She was a single parent for 6 years before her current marriage. Sandy resides in Spring, Texas with her husband, 18-year-old son, and two large dogs. Their 28-year-old son is in AA and doing very well. She and her husband have been faithful members of Al-Anon for more than five years and are committed for a lifetime to the program because of the impact they have seen on others in the program and the lives Al-Anon has changed. To quote Sandy, "the program has saved and changed our lives for sure."

Dealing with Sadness or Grief after a Loss

It's hard to lose someone or something you care about. This is true even if you think you're prepared. Feeling sadness, anger, anxiety, or grief after a loss is something most people experience in life. However, reactions to loss can vary a great deal from person to person.

Knowing a little more about types of loss and common reactions can help. It's also important to know how to take care of yourself in times of grief. Sometimes, the very process of reaching out and telling others what you need can be helpful in and of itself. Grief is personal. Below are some information that can help you while going through a loss.

Common Losses People Grieve

People grieve for many different reasons. Some examples of these include loss of:

- a loved one,
- a pet,
- a beloved public figure, leader, or mentor,
- a life role, such as a career change (e.g., transitioning out of the military),
- physical ability,
- relationship due to divorce or separation,
- home, neighborhood, or friends when moving,

- life's potential and dreams,
- possessions, or
- belief in a person, idea or cause.

For veterans, grief may come from loss of:

- a military comrade who died in battle (veterans may also experience survivor guilt, a sense of remorse for having survived when others did not),
- sense of closeness that was had with fellow service members,
- identity as a member of the armed forces,
- physical ability (e.g., disability acquired during service, traumatic brain injury, etc.), or
- mental health (e.g., PTSD, loss of sense of safety).

Expressions of Grief

Grief is personal. Everyone responds differently to loss. Some people show grief in a way that can be seen and felt by people around them. Others do not. It's important not to assume that something is wrong if you or someone you know doesn't outwardly mourn. It simply means the loss is being handled in a different way.

You might experience some of these common reactions:

- Physical—stomachache or headache, pain around the heart area, insomnia, fatigue, dizziness, trembling, panic attacks.
- Emotional—shock, disbelief, numbness, anxiety, confusion, frustration, depression, guilt, loneliness, anger, detachment.

- Behavioral—crying, pacing, staring, forgetting things, loss of interest, poor focus, too much or too little sleep, isolating, obsessing over the loss, worrying about one's own health.
- Spiritual—anger at God or a higher power, losing faith, finding faith, becoming more thoughtful or philosophical.

Grief is a Process

Feelings can come and go. You might find yourself denying the loss happened. At other times, you might feel sadness or a range of other feelings. You might notice yourself feeling angry with the person for dying or leaving, angry at yourself, or angry at someone else.

You might have feelings of relief or moments of happiness. At times, it can be hard to accept the loss and you might find yourself bargaining ("If only I…"). It's good to know there is no correct way to grieve. With time, most people find they are able to come to terms with their loss.

Self-Care While Grieving

Taking care of yourself can help you through the process of grieving. Here are some tips:

- Let yourself grieve. Take time to experience the feelings that come with the loss. Let emotions come and go. This emotional pain can be very hard, but it's a basic part of healing.

- Talk about your experience. People may not know what you're going through. Talk to people you trust, at work and home, and let them know how to support you. Find someone who will listen without judgment. This might be a family member or friend, a chaplain or other spiritual counselor, a therapist, a fellow veteran, or a support group.
- Keep busy. Do purposeful work that is consistent with your values.
- Exercise. Any bit of exercise can help, even just going for a short walk. Make a plan to get some form of exercise daily.
- Eat well. During times of distress, your body needs good food more than ever. Good nutrition can help you feel better physically and emotionally.
- Wait to make major decisions. Loss often involves unwanted or unexpected changes. Think about taking time to grieve before making major changes, such as selling your home or changing jobs.
- Record your thoughts in a journal. If you like to write, journaling can help. But if you find you feel worse after journaling, then stop and try another way of getting out your feelings.
- Take advantage of your spiritual or religious beliefs. You may find it helpful to call upon your spiritual beliefs to cope with your loss. Prayer or services, for instance, may be helpful. You might consult with a chaplain or pastoral counselor.
- Get professional help if needed. If you find that, over a period of time, your grief continues to interfere with your ability to move forward with your life, consider seeking help. Counseling through your EAP or other veteran services may be available to you.

- o You can meet with other veterans to talk about grief or other concerns at your local vet center: http://www.vetcenter.va.gov/index.asp
- o VA medical center locations can be found here: http://www.va.gov/landing2_locations.htm
- o Information about chaplaincy services available through the VA is available here: http://www1.va.gov/chaplain/
- o Veterans in crisis and their loved ones can call the Veterans Crisis Line, 1-800-273-8255, and press 1.

• You likely have strategies that you have found helpful when you experienced a loss in the past. Utilize the strategies that work best for you.

Source: https://www.va.gov/vetsinworkplace/docs/em_eap_dealing_loss.asp

I Am No One

Allison T.

I am no one. Nobody. I am inconsequential. I hold no value. Oh, I am valued and needed, but I hold no value. If I held value, people couldn't use me for their purposes. I would not allow them to use me as their excuse or reason for doing the horrible things they do. They hurt people—me, themselves, and others. And it is my fault. Of course it was. They told me so, and I did not say or do anything to stop them.

If I held value, people would not be able to recognize that I am a pushover. A people pleaser. You want the dirty work, tedious tasks, or the mundane, everyday chores pushed onto someone other than yourself? Ask me to do it. Of course I will do it! I want you to see that I am capable of doing something right or good. I can bring value to your life by doing these things for you, and you will be happy. But I have no value.

If I held value, people could not have used my body for their pleasure. If I did, the ongoing sexual abuse since I was 4 perpetrated on my body by neighbors and relatives as well as those while I was in college and my husband would have killed me. (Yes, he is an alcoholic and raped me often. When he was too drunk in his attempts, he blamed me for not loving him or for no longer being attractive.) But I didn't die.

I was no one. Nobody. It did not matter that I took on so much to please others that I am constantly worn-out. It did not matter that the very little feelings I felt were squashed to a point that I could not even recognize what it is I felt. Do you know that a person can live about 40 days without food, about 3 days without water, about eight minutes without air *but* only about one second without *hope*?

In 2001, my husband and I had been married 10 hard long years. Year one, I got my first of many ultimatums that would end in divorce if I did not do as he asked. Divorce was not an option for me. One, God hates divorce. Two, I loved him, and three, a divorce would have proven my parents correct that I am a failure. This was also the year I started my first job since leaving the military in 1992. And it was the year my husband took his threat of divorce to a higher level by informing my mom before he said anything to me. My parents have just been informed that I failed as a wife. My husband, who was never happy with me, appeared to finally be ready to act on his threat of divorce.

I tried to get questions answered. He would only yell and tell me it is all my doing. My head was spinning; I couldn't think straight. I just wanted this be over! How could I make this all stop! I lost my hope. And then the words came out: "It's just going to be better if I'm dead." With that, I ran to my closet that locked from the inside and where I had a gun. I could only think about getting it out. I could also only think about what others would think of what I did, not me. But that saved me. I could not imagine putting my children through something so horrific. I made the choice to live for them.

Still, I was nothing but a piece of meat, and this was another big bite among so many other bite marks of differing sizes and shapes. I divorced my husband after 23 years of marriage. I enabled his drunken behaviors by accepting and excusing him with forgiveness because he did not know what he was doing. I was the only one to remember on the next day. Then one day, he scared me. He was behaving as if drunk but was sober. He has scared me lots of times. This time that he was sober, I was really afraid of what he might be capable of doing to me. Somewhere in these past years, God had brought me to a place of having self-worth and recognizing some of my value. The night he left, I recommitted my life to Christ. Shortly after my divorce, I started attending a new church, and I truly felt growth with Jesus and no one else on the throne of my heart.

This is the life I cannot lose. I am finally somebody defined by my identity in Christ. I am a new creation. And I know that with all I went through, He is using me to help others. Quoting from Philippians 1:6, "For I am confident of this very thing, that He who began a good work in you will perfect it until the day of Christ Jesus." I thank God for today and cannot wait to live the rest of my story. I am alive! Galatians has only six chapters, and these passages hold special meaning for me:

1:10—I am to *not* live for the approval of others.

2:20—I am *not* defined by my past.

3:27—I *am* worthy in Christ not by anything I do.

4:7—I *am* a child of God, *not* a slave to others.

5:25—I am to *not* react to my feelings and emotions, but *be led* by the Spirit.

6:9—I will *not* tire of doing good in Christ.

How I Went from Desperately Wanting to Kill Myself to Loving Every Minute of My Life

Sondi Jones

Art Linkletter says the darndest things. Yes, I know. It's supposed to be "Kids say the darndest things." But for purposes of this story, I'm sticking with Art Linkletter saying the darndest things. My daddy looked like Art's twin. The better looking of the two, Art was a good man. Daddy was a compulsive liar. He sounded like Art. He even took a breath like Art before he told his joke, story, or lie. I always loved to listen to Daddy's stories. Sometimes I knew it was an over-the-top story. Mother used to say it was easier for Daddy to tell a lie than the truth.

Daddy and Mother got married in 1933. She was pregnant. Mother even told me my brother was conceived on the courthouse steps in Muleshoe, Texas. She was 17 years old, 9 months older than Daddy. Too young to get married even in those days. Daddy was an alcoholic from the start of their marriage. Mother was a stay-at-home housewife. She just cleaned, and cleaned, and cleaned. Did I say cleaned? Mother was the cleanest person I ever knew.

My two brothers were both born in Muleshoe, Texas: Jack, who was 10 years older than me, and Bob, who was 7 years older than me. The family moved to Long Beach, California, where I was born. When I was 15 months old, my brother, Jack, got rheumatic fever. The doctors advised my parents to move him to a drier climate. As it happened, my grandparents on my mother's side lived in Tucson, Arizona at that time. That's where I was raised.

From what I was told, Daddy quit drinking for about 5 years. But I guess they still had their ups and downs. Daddy was a womanizer. Remember I said he looked just like Art Linkletter, the good-looking one. When I was in first grade, each day I would walk past a certain house and the radio would be on. I could hear *Kids Say the Darndest Things* with Art Linkletter coming from the woman's kitchen. I loved Art then.

I don't know why, but I worshipped my daddy. I thought Daddy could do anything and everything. He could fix everything and always be there. I don't know where those ideas came from. None of it was true. He never had time for us kids. One day, I asked Daddy to take me to the zoo. Jokingly, he asked me, "Why would you want to go to the zoo? We have a bunch of monkeys right here." Daddy never took me to the zoo, but he still looked like Art Linkletter.

Daddy and Mother divorced in 1952. I was almost 8 years old. I missed my daddy so much. Through all the stress, I lost my hair. The doctor my mother took me to gave her a green salve to put on my bare scalp every day. Of course, the kids at school made fun of me. God, forgive them for they knew not what they were doing. I failed the third grade that year. After that, school was always hard for me. School was the last thing on my mind.

I remember my aunt coming over to get my mother to go out dancing for three Saturdays in a row. The third time, she warned Mother, saying that she and her friend, Joan, would throw her into the car next time. My mother was saying, "I am going to stay here and raise Sondra." First time, Mother had a beer. Second time, she had two. Third week, three. After that, she was ready to go dancing, and she was good at it.

Mother was a cute, petite, pretty lady with snappy dark brown eyes, and dark-brown, almost black, hair. She was 4'10" and 97 pounds. An hourglass figure, a real head turner. Mother had no problems finding a male friend. She never brought them home, as she was overprotective of me. Thank you, Jesus!

Mother had never been a drinker, but she started drinking at this time and became an alcoholic by the time I was 8 years old. I was totally independent. No one knew where I was or what I was doing. I'd be riding my bike home at 11:00 or 11:30 pm. Who cared? Nobody! I could have had the whole football team over for tea and no one would have known or cared. No one!

Mother always rented us a small one-bedroom house. I slept with Mother until I got married. She always came home after the bar closed at 2:00 am. Every three days, I'd go to the bar for money for a hamburger, fries, and a strawberry shake.

It only took about two years for Mother to become a full-fledged alcoholic, a happy drunk. By this time, Jack, my older brother, was out of the service, married, and living in California. He was the only Santa I ever had. Bob ran away from home at 13 years old and never came back. Jack ended up working for Lockheed Aerospace. Bob was a rodeo clown and a bull rider.

By this time, I was an independent 10-year-old. No one ever knew or cared where I was except for Jack, but he was in California. I would be riding my bike home at 10:30 pm or later from my friend's house. It was about a 3-mile ride and nobody cared.

Thank you, Jesus, for watching over me when I didn't even know you were there. By now, Mother was at the bar 365 days a year. If I wanted to see Mother at Christmas or Easter, I always went to the bar for a potluck. During the other times, I went to get money for a hamburger, fries, and a strawberry shake. Mother or some damn drunk would give me the money. But I would be back in three days. I'd be hungry again. I know... I just repeated myself. But, damn it, I was hungry. I was so shy and sad. If I wrote a book about my life, no one would believe it. They would think it was fiction. Including me!

Once, when I was 14, I got to spend a Saturday night with my grandma on my mother's side. Another old lady friend of my grandma's came over. We played beauty parlor. I dolled them all up for church the next day. I rolled their hair, painted their nails, put their feet in a pan of water, and shaved their legs.

The next week, Grandma, who was chronically depressed, committed suicide. She took Drano. It burned her from the inside out. Even though she was a White person, she looked like a Black person in the casket. I don't think you go to hell if you're sick, and Grandma was *sick*. There she was. She went to heaven with my red nail polish on.

I would like to tell you a little bit about me. When I was born, my mother named me Sondra. But my birth certificate spelled my name Sandra. She never changed it. So I started off on the wrong foot from day one. Eventually, I found out that Mother tried to abort me at 5 months. That was never a good feeling.

The years went by and life happened. I got married and divorced. Somehow, I survived. When I married my second husband, I already had a son, and I was so dysfunctional. One night, we had an argument about my son, Wayne. Bill asked me to let him take over, let him take care of Wayne and me. I don't know what came over me, but at that very second, I gave in. I was so tired of being independent. I guess that's when I became codependent. We did everything together. We even wore our hair alike. He was my best friend.

We moved to Corpus Christi, Texas, his hometown. That's where we had our first Christmas together. One night before Christmas, my mother-in-law kept taking Bill's brothers to the back bedroom. Boy, did I go off on her! I let her know that if she had anything to say about me, she should say it to my face! Well, it turned out, she was showing them what she had bought me for Christmas. What did I know about Christmas with a family!

As the years went by and our family grew, I came to love Bill totally and completely. When he had an affair, I practically stopped living. I got down to 83 pounds and looked 90 years old. I was lost. I had had the rug yanked out from under me. I cried nonstop for two years. I even slept sitting up. It was too painful lying down. There is no pain like a broken heart. I wanted to go crazy. I wanted to kill myself.

I always felt that when I was in my car alone, everyone knew my husband had left me for another woman. I was so ashamed, always with a lump in my throat ready to cry. I couldn't take it any longer. I knew suicide was my only way out. I hurt so badly. It was always on my mind. I missed my husband so, so, so much.

When you are in this state of mind, you are not thinking of your loved ones, the ones you leave behind. I just lived in my bedroom. I had to get a job. When I was not at work, I was in my bedroom crying.

Eventually, finally, the moment came. I knew I had to do it or quit thinking about it. I went into the bathroom with razor in hand. I heard the front door. It was my son, Wayne. He ran in to get something and ran right out. I had a balcony off my bedroom. I hurried to the door, opened it, and hollered to my son, *"Don't forget. I love you!"* When he turned around, running backward, he had the most beautiful smile on his face. I can still see it. I never saw that smile before or since. We were hollering who loved the other the most.

"No, I love you more."

"No, I love you more!"

Until he was out of sight.

Nevertheless, I returned to the bathroom to complete the job with the razor I had. Then my best friend, Susie, knocked on the door. She came to check on me. She knew how depressed I was. She caught me in the act. She was always so funny. She said, "Sondi, you won't even let me move to Iowa. I'll be damned if I let you go to hell." We both laughed. The spell was broken.

Well, I guess by now, you're wondering what happened to me. I started seeing a therapist. Through him, I became aware that I was not crying for Bill. I was crying for the little girl that was abandoned by her daddy. Bill did not do this to me. I did it to myself.

One time at a church group, we were studying a book by Beth Moore. We were going to watch a movie, pray, and break our emotional chains. I wanted to leave. After arguing with a lady in the group, she promised I could leave if I couldn't handle it. I made her promise not to stop me.

Thank God I stayed. I heard God tell me it wasn't me my mother was trying to get rid of. It was my daddy. She was tired of his ways. Daddy and mother divorced when I was about seven years old.

I am now 75 years young. My 2 sons, Wayne and Troy, and daughter, Allison, are doing well. I have 7 grandchildren and 4 great-grandchildren. I have a beautiful little house, and a little yard for all my flowers. I belong to every organization in Tomball, Texas. Ever heard of that town? It's on the map, I promise. I have so many friends whom I love, and they love me back. I go where I want, with who I want, when I want. And I am in control of the remote! LOL.

I believe God was watching over me my whole life. I believe in God's perfect timing when he sent my son and my friend,

Susie, at just the right moment. I am alive and happy today. I love my life. I have no complaints. I am so very thankful and grateful to be alive!

Keeping Your Children Alive and Happy Through Their School Years

By J. Adams

Unfortunately, sadly, many of our beautiful, wonderful children are killing themselves or going into deep depression and missing out on life because of being bullied in school, often through social media or the Internet.

As of this writing, I am 76 years old, so neither I nor my two children experienced such bullying while growing up. However, it is definitely something my daughter, with two children aged 18 and 16, had had to look at, learn about, and deal with in many *different* ways. For the most part, bullies no longer smack you, try to push you down, or steal your money or homework. Instead they hurt people's feelings by exaggerating very minor events, telling lies about you, and making fun of you all on social media and the Internet. However, the negative effects of victimization from a bully has kids reacting in all kinds of ways from anger and tears to social withdrawal, depression, physical injury, addiction, self-harm, and even suicide.

While I am, of course, aware of much of what went on in my daughter's family over the years and how she handled and worked with many of the problems and issues they went through, when I told her I wanted to write about the problem of cyberbullying, how she dealt with it and how she suggested all parents work with it, we sat down together and talked for several hours. What I offer you in this article is from my experience raising two children, what I have gleaned from TV and the computer about cyberbullying, *and* what I learned from her in our 3-hour talk a few days ago.

Talking with your children as they are growing up is *very, very, very* important. It includes *listening* to them and *talking* with them in ways they can understand and know that you really care. So how do you do that? What do I mean by that?

As your children are growing up, include them in all important conversations: money, care of the house, family and personal responsibilities, what not to watch on TV and why, movies, and video games. If you watch the news on TV, include them in your conversations about it. When talking with them, be conscious of their age and pay attention to what they can and cannot understand. Always make sure they understand that you are talking with them in a very straight and purposeful way because you love them so very much. You want them to grow up happy, healthy, and wise. Let them know that frequently.

So what is there to talk about? Sadly, many children in the United States grow up watching violent movies on TV with their parents as well as watching them play violent video games. Sometimes they are allowed to play some of these games as well even before their teen years. Unfortunately, this allows the child or a young person to become desensitized to other people's feelings. They don't always realize what they are doing when they post upsetting pictures or messages about someone on social media.

My daughter said she never let her children watch PG-13 and R-rated movies until they were of the right age to do so, except, she said, on very few rare occasions. Even when they were very close to being the right age, she always discussed the movie with them afterward. You know your child and what he or she can handle emotionally. Always be mindful of that when deciding what movies they are allowed to watch.

Use parental controls on TV, computers, and phones and then keep up with it all. As a responsible, caring parent, you must keep up with what your children are sending, receiving, and viewing. Know that kids can find ways around it. You must watch out for that. Also make sure your children understand that you are keeping up with all their social media because you love them so very much and you don't want anything bad happening to them or being posted about them.

Also my daughter has all necessary names and passwords. That way, she can keep up with what they are posting and what they are viewing. Of course, she does not check their sites every day. She does not have time for that, and she understands that they are entitled to a certain amount of privacy as well. She also depends on them to tell her whenever they have a concern. But she does scan their sites occasionally just to keep an eye on everything. Also having the necessary names and passwords provide her with an extra way of contacting them if needed, and the children understand this.

Be open about talking with them about everything, and then it is much easier to block certain things on their computers and phones.

Every child needs to be involved in something beyond their classes, like a club, theater, sports, etc. Then they have a different group of friends, but you still need to talk with them about it. If possible, involve other family members. Children need them also.

As a parent, you must talk with your children straight and clear and with great love. However, no matter how wonderful and loving a parent you are, there are times you child will be very unhappy about something or several things. If they want to talk about it, be a good listener. If they don't, then allow them their space with patience and understanding. You can be a good friend to them, but you must also—and most importantly—be their parent in the process. Be their parent both at home and wherever you may be.

The important thing, then, is to talk with your child in a way he or she can hear and understand. And then listen, *really listen* to them. Know who their friends are, what clubs they are in, what they are doing after school, what classes they are taking in school, and how it's going. How happy or unhappy is your child with his or her life in general? Do you know their friends, and how happy are they with those friendships? It is very important to know all the details so you can make sure that no matter what upsets or problems your child may go through, you are there supporting him or her in every way possible. You are there for them. And they know it. That makes all the difference and is the key to their happiness.

Military Sexual Trauma

Overview

The term "military sexual trauma" (MST) commonly refers to sexual assault or harassment experienced during military service. MST includes any sexual activity that you are involved with against your will. Examples include:

- being pressured or coerced into sexual activities, such as with threats of negative treatment if you refuse to cooperate or with promises of better treatment in exchange for sex;
- someone having sexual contact with you without your consent, such as when you were asleep or intoxicated;
- being physically forced to have sex;
- being touched in a sexual way that made you uncomfortable;
- repeated comments about your body or sexual activities; and
- threatening and unwanted sexual advances.

Anyone can experience MST regardless of gender. Like other types of trauma, MST can negatively affect a person's mental and physical health even many years later. Things you may experience could include:

- disturbing memories or nightmares;
- difficulty feeling safe;
- feelings of depression or numbness;

- problems with alcohol or other drugs;
- feeling isolated from other people;
- problems with anger, irritability, or other strong emotions;
- issues with sleep; and
- physical health problems

How Common is MST?

An estimated 1 in 4 female veterans and 1 in 100 male veterans in the VA healthcare system report experiencing MST. It is important to note that by percentage, women are at greater risk of MST, but nearly 40 percent of veterans who disclose MST to VA are men.

What Are the Symptoms Associated with MST?

- Post-traumatic stress disorder (PTSD) and other psychological health issues—Sexual assault survivors in both the military and civilian populations show a higher lifetime rate of PTSD for both men (65 percent) and women (49.5 percent). VA medical record data indicates that, in addition to PTSD, the diagnoses most frequently associated with MST among users of VA health care are depression and other mood disorders and substance use disorders.
- Difficulty with relationships and social functioning—Veterans who have experienced MST may report difficulties with interpersonal relationships. In some cases, the abuse triggers trust issues, problems engaging in social activities, and possible difficulties with sexual

dysfunction. It is also common to experience emotional challenges with guilt, shame, and anger over the trauma. Many survivors also report difficulties finding or maintaining work after their military service.
- Physical health problems—MST survivors may suffer from sexual difficulties, chronic pain, weight or eating problems, or gastrointestinal problems. Additionally, they may experience difficulty with attention, concentration, and memory and have trouble staying focused or frequently finding their mind wandering.
- Substance abuse—Drug and alcohol abuse has a higher correlation among sexual assault survivors than among non-victims. Studies have found that drug use—including marijuana, cocaine, and other illicit substances—is up to 10 times as high for victims of sexual assault.
- Additional medical and mental health conditions—There is a strong association with MST survivors in developing certain specific medical conditions (such as obesity or weight loss, chronic pulmonary disease, liver disease, and hypothyroidism) and mental health conditions (such as bipolar disorders, schizophrenia, eating disorders, and post-traumatic stress disorder).

Does MST have to control the veteran?

There are ways to cope with MST that empower a veteran to take control of the symptoms resulting from their trauma. Some of those coping mechanisms are outlined below:

- Professional help—There is no shame in asking for help with your symptoms associated with MST or

PTSD. It does not make you weak. It takes strength to ask for help. Seeking a counselor or therapist who specializes in sexual trauma can be a good first step to healing. If you have experienced MST during your military career, you can also find a Veterans Service Organization (VSO) benefits expert to discuss filing a claim with VA. All VSO benefits experts are veterans themselves (some are also survivors of MST), and they can help walk you through the claims process with compassion and discretion. Also every VA facility has a designated MST coordinator who serves as a contact person for MST-related issues. This person is your advocate and can help you find and access VA services and programs, state and federal benefits, and community resources.

- Lifestyle changes—Interacting with other trauma survivors and other veterans who have experience with MST, exercising, eating healthy, volunteering, avoiding drugs and alcohol, spending more time with loved ones, and practicing optimism are all helpful.
- Mindfulness—To be mindful is to be aware of and to be able to concentrate on the present. It can be breathing exercises or focusing on a singular thing in your present, like the taste of a piece of chocolate or coffee but intensely focusing on that one thing.
- Practicing optimism—Hunt for the good stuff in your life, the things that create joy and a sense of peace or happiness. At some point in your day, reflect on the good things that have happened to you in the last 24 hours. It can be as small as finding your favorite ink pen or celebrating the birth of a child, whatever brings you joy.

- Peer groups—Finding others who have experienced MST can help you feel comfortable talking about MST and working through the intense emotions associated with it.
- Emotional support animals—Many veterans who struggle with MST have adopted emotional support animals, usually dogs who help veterans feel more at ease and comfortable in situations that may otherwise cause them undue stress.
- Exploring the options—There are many different ways to regain control. Those that work for you may not work for someone else, and those that work for someone else may not work for you. Exploring the different options and being open-minded to new and potential solutions is helpful.

If you are having current difficulties related to MST, the VA is there to support you in whatever way will help you best from simply learning more about how MST affects people to getting treatment that helps you cope with how MST is impacting your life currently or if you prefer, treatment that involves discussing your experiences in more depth.

How Can I Get Help for MST through the VA?

- Speak with your existing VA health care provider
- Contact the MST coordinator or the Women Veterans Program manager at your local VA medical center
- Contact your local Vet Center
- Call 1-800-827-1000, VA's general benefit information hotline

Sources:

DAV. "Military Sexual Trauma—MST." 2019. https://tinyurl.com/tdo8tep.

VA. "Military Sexual Trauma." 2020. https://tinyurl.com/uxl7929.

What is Moral Injury?

> Moral injury is the damage done to one's conscience or moral compass when that person perpetrates, witnesses, or fails to prevent acts that transgress one's own moral beliefs, values, or ethical codes of conduct.

Within the context of military service, particularly regarding the experience of war, "moral injury" refers to the lasting emotional, psychological, social, behavioral, and spiritual impacts of actions that violate a service member's core moral values and behavioral expectations of self or others. Moral injury almost always pivots with the dimension of time. Moral codes evolve alongside identities, and transitions inform perspectives that form new conclusions about old events.

While the concept itself is not new—throughout history philosophers, poets, and warriors themselves have long wrestled with the ethical dilemmas inherent in war—the term moral injury is more recent as the aftermath of war zone trauma.

Moral injury is increasingly a focus of discussion and study across disciplines and settings. Returning veterans and those who care for them are struggling to understand and respond effectively when experiences of war result in levels of anguish, anger, and alienation not well explained in terms of mental health diagnoses such as post-traumatic stress disorder (PTSD). Multiple deployments to Afghanistan and Iraq have exacerbated the problems active duty military and separated veterans experience.

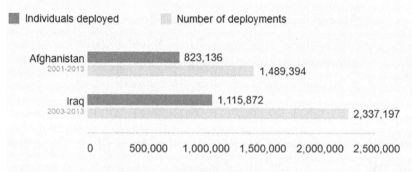

Source: U.S. Department of Defense

Examples of Moral Injury in War

- Using deadly force in combat and causing the harm or death of civilians knowingly but without alternatives or accidentally
- Giving orders in combat that result in the injury or death of a fellow service member
- Failing to provide medical aid to an injured civilian or service member
- Returning home from deployment and hearing of the executions of cooperating local nationals
- Failing to report knowledge of a sexual assault or rape committed against oneself, a fellow service member, or civilians
- Following orders that were illegal, immoral, and against the rules of engagement (ROE) or Geneva Convention

- A change in belief about the necessity or justification for war during or after one's service

What Are the Consequences of Moral Injury?

Moral injury can lead to serious distress, depression, and suicidal tendency. Moral injury can take the life of those suffering from it both metaphorically and literally. Moral injury debilitates people, preventing them from living full and healthy lives.

The effects of moral injury go beyond the individual and can destroy one's capacity to trust others, impinging on the family system and the larger community. Moral injury must be brought forward into the community for a shared process of healing. In the context of a soul, with respect to the diversity of beliefs and religious perspectives held by those involved with moral injury, consider this: Moral injury is damage done to the soul of the individual. War is one (but not the only) thing that can cause this damage. Abuse, rape, and violence may cause similar types of damage. "Soul repair" and "soul wound" are terms already in use by researchers and institutions in the United States who are exploring moral injury and pathways to recovery.

Why Haven't We Heard about This Before?

Traumatic brain injury (TBI) and post-traumatic stress disorder (PTS or PTSD) became household terms over the last decade thanks to the maturation of attitudes about the costs of war. Moral injury is now the object of growing focus by researchers and academics in the same manner.

Moral injury does not, by its nature, present itself immediately. Some will experience questions of moral injury days after an incident. For many others, difficulties will not surface for years. An experience with potential for moral injury is typically realized after a change in personal moral codes or belief systems.

What Should We Do about Moral Injury?

Moral injury must be acknowledged in the same way that we acknowledge the physical and mental costs of traumas experienced in war and other place of danger. Moral injury is subjective and personal. Research on moral injury is younger than research on PTSD. The definitions, ideas, and practices Syracuse University is working with are both experimental and varied.

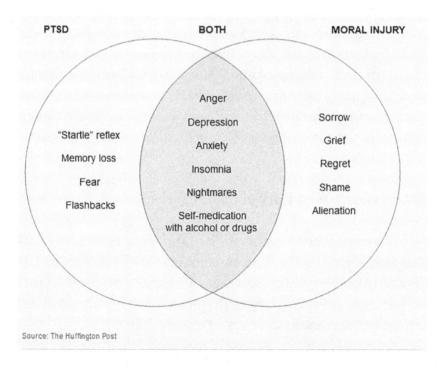

Source: The Huffington Post

Traumas of a type and severity that cause PTSD are likely to cause moral injury too. This does not mean treating PTSD will "treat" moral injury or vice versa. Syracuse's Moral Injury Project favors the tenet that "treatment" of moral injury must be defined by the individual according to their beliefs and needs. Outlets for acknowledging and confronting moral injury include talk therapy (peer support groups or one-on-one counseling), religious dialogue, art, writing, spiritual gatherings, and more.

Therapists, counselors, social workers, and clergy are often at the front lines of addressing moral injury; however, the larger community can also take part. Consider that moral injury affects and is affected by the moral codes across a community. In the case of military veterans, moral injury stems in part from feelings of isolation from civilian society. Moral injury then is a burden carried by very few until the "outsiders" become aware of and interested in sharing it. Listening and witnessing to moral injury outside the confines of a clinical setting can be a way to break the silence that so often surrounds moral injury.

*PTSD is a clinical diagnosis, identified and treated according to criteria and methods prescribed by the American Psychiatric Association (APA). The APA last updated its Diagnostic and Statistical Manual of Mental Disorders (DSM-5) in 2013. Moral injury does not yet have a DSM-5 code akin to PTS.

Sources:

1. David Wood, "Moral Injury—The Grunts," *Huffington Post,* March 28, 2014.
2. The Moral Injury Project. http://moralinjuryproject.syr.edu/about-moral-injury/.

Learning War and Reconciliation

A sermon delivered by the Rev. David Peters

"And they shall beat their swords into plowshares, and their spears into pruning hooks; nation shall not lift up sword against nation, neither shall they learn war anymore."

War is not easy to learn. It does not come naturally to any of us, least of all to me, a bookish teenager whose only sport was soccer and who was afraid to go canoeing. At the age of 15, when I felt a calling to the ministry, I knew I needed to toughen up. So the day after I graduated from high school, I was up at zero dark thirty to take a bus to Parris Island, South Carolina to go to Marine Corps boot camp.

I learned war that summer. The men I entered boot camp with were mostly teenagers like me. We learned how to march, salute, and polish brass and boots. It seemed we were always polishing something. Mars, the god of war, is vain, flashy, and showy to a fault. But this wasn't war. War is killing, and killing is a skill you have to learn.

Signs on the side of our barracks read "More sweat in peace, less blood in war" and "Your endurance is limited by your consciousness and your willingness to go on." These were our scriptures. We motivated one another, and the drill instructors motivated us. They would get in our faces and shout, "You can quit when I quit!"

I fixed a bayonet to my M16 rifle and practiced the almost liturgical movements in step with the drill instructor's command. Pointy end toward the enemy and "thrust"! We executed as one, imagining, and not imagining, the bones of our enemies breaking, a sound you never forget. My DI was always grabbing us by the helmet, giving it a shake, and looking right into our eyes screaming, "Let me see your war face!" You can teach killing, and you can teach war, and I was an avid student there in the hot sands of Parris Island.

They put us in pits with boxing gloves, and when the whistle blew, we started in on one another. We pummeled one another in 60 seconds of combat. For those 60 seconds, we had to channel every ounce of rage, bitterness, hate. We had to survive any way we could. When the whistle blew to stop us, we continued to throw punches. They always had to shove us away from one another. The DI said to us, "Use everything you have in a fight—a helmet, a shovel, your hands. Never back down, and never surrender." We learned hand-to-hand combat for war. We learned how to kill a man, a person, with our hands. "Use everything you have in a fight, never back down, never surrender." Even if we, like the prophet, had longed for the day when we beat our swords into plowshares, that activity was not authorized by the United States Marine Corps.

War is hard to learn, but it sticks with you. Being a warrior is like being a priest with its own vestments, rituals, and beliefs. You never lose it no matter how old or kind or gentle you grow with time. And when I think about it, we really didn't learn to *do* war, we learned to *be* war. But that was a long time ago.

You and I know what happened on *this* day. On *that* day, the end of days. Many of you were right here or somewhere near here. You smelled it. Nothing smells like it. You know what I mean.

I had been out of the Marine Corps for a couple of years when 9/11 happened. I had just finished seminary and was working as a youth minister at a church in Pennsylvania. Pretty peaceful activities mostly, except for the occasional paintball trip with the youth group.

After *that* day. After the world changed for us. After we invaded Afghanistan and Iraq—yes, it was us—we did this. Only a few people, usually young men, *did* it. Only a few young men and women are ever on the "tip of the spear." But the whole nation, all of us, pushed the shaft of that spear into the enemy. Maybe we're way in the back of the shaft or up toward the front, but we're all pushing, one way or another.

Shortly after the invasion, I realized thousands of young women and men, just a little older than the kids in my youth group, were heading into a long war. I knew they would need chaplains, someone to bring God's grace in a place that didn't have much of either. So I signed up as an army chaplain, just a few weeks after the invasion. I was 27, just married, a new parent with another one on the way. I was the second youngest chaplain in the army. I was also way older than almost all my soldiers.

On every September 11, in Iraq, and on every army base I've served on, there would be a 9/11 memorial ceremony. A general or a colonel would always say to us, "We're here in Iraq today fighting the same people who attacked us on that Tuesday morning." It was a simple connection for the military. We army folks, at least, are simple people.

You have to keep things simple in a war. You have to know the rules. In war, we call these rules the rules of engagement or the ROE. These are the rules that govern when you can use deadly force. In Iraq, when I was there, you could kill anyone whom you felt was a threat to you or someone else. We all had the ultimate power, the power to take a life. You never forget what it's like to have the power and *be* the one who kills another human. "Use everything you have in a fight, never back down, never surrender."

Rules of engagement or the ROE. That's what Peter wants to know in our gospel reading. "What are the rules?" he asks. "Lord, how many times may my brother sin against me and I *have* to forgive him?" But Jesus doesn't give him a rule. Jesus refuses to make reconciliation simple, formulaic, or easily reproducible in a power point slide or in a sermon delivered in a beautiful church on 9/11.

I'm an Iraq veteran, and one thing I've found is that most combat veterans I know have very little anger or hatred toward the "insurgents," the men who tried to kill us in Iraq or Afghanistan. Those men were just doing their jobs, and we were just doing ours. But no. Our anger is more personal. Anger usually is.

My brother and sister veterans have been used in beer commercials, at country music concerts, and on carefully built stages in the shadow of our capitol or the buildings of this city. Sometimes this makes us angry.

We also have some anger at the self-obsessed nation we came home to—anger at the God who was on our side, anger at ourselves for not doing a better job, anger at our husband or wife for finding someone else while we were gone, anger for losing a war, anger for letting people in our team die, anger for not bringing everyone home, and anger for being powerless after we had the power of the gods.

The hardest person to forgive is a brother or sister or a friend. The most difficult person to reconcile with is someone close who betrayed you, sold you out, or hurt you. Peter knows this, and that's why he asks it this way. Peter doesn't ask how many times he has to forgive the Romans or the Greeks or

Herod. He asks how many times he has to forgive a member of the church. In the Greek it's literally, *his brother*.

It's astounding how difficult reconciliation can be. We are smart people here today. We may have been challenged in life. We may have been successful. We know how to *do* things. But we are often just as childish as Peter who asks this question, "What is the bare minimum that I must *do*? What is the smallest number of times I'm required to forgive?"

But Jesus makes it clear. You don't *do* forgiveness. You have to *be* forgiveness. You don't *do* reconciliation. You must *be* reconciliation. Just like you, the Marine Corps didn't just teach me to *do* war. They taught me to *be* war. We have to *learn to be* reconciliation.

Jesus taught it to Peter with this story of the unforgiving servant. The unforgiving servant in Jesus's story is reconciled to the king and forgiven of his debt not because he made amends, not because he cleaned up his act, and not because he changed his ways. He is reconciled to the king and forgiven because the king gives him grace freely and without any strings attached. The king is not stingy with his forgiveness to the servant just as God is not miserly with us. Jesus tells us, in this story, that the heart of God beats with mercy, mercy, mercy, mercy.

The God revealed to us in Jesus Christ does not dole out small portions of reconciliation to the worthy. Our God of abundance overflows with forgiveness, love, mercy, and reconciliation above what is deserved or merited. And that is where reconciliation starts—with this recognition of our own reconciliation. But it ends there for this unforgiving servant. He goes out into the street after he's been forgiven and chokes a man who owes him $100. He doesn't get it. He doesn't understand that if we put a cloud of revenge and unforgiveness over the head of some other person, that same cloud is big and hangs over our head too. He grabs his enemy with a death grip, and revenge whispers in his ear, "Use everything you have in a fight, never back down, never surrender."

When I came home from Iraq, it took me a long time to find reconciliation. I was so angry at myself, at my ex-wife, at the army, and the God I went to war with. I remember kneeling in a church in Philadelphia with a girlfriend next to me. When the general confession started—our opportunity for reconciliation—I refused to say the words, "We confess that we have sinned against you." I muttered under my breath, "God, I'll confess my sins against you when you confess your sins against me." It took me a long time to *be* reconciled.

Reconciliation, for me, came in little movements and big moments. It came when I realized my choke hold on my enemies was a choke hold on myself too. Reconciliation came when I abandoned the mantra I learned in war, "Use everything you have in a fight, never back down, never surrender," and I surrendered to a God who loved me and a Savior who was with me in my darkest hour. It came when I was honest about my anger with God, and I confessed that out loud to a priest as we read the words from page 449 in the Prayer Book: The Reconciliation of a Penitent: "Have mercy on me, O God, according to your loving kindness."

Today, Jesus may be calling us to give up "trying harder to do reconciliation." We have to *be* it. Jesus was. He was reconciliation. As our prayer says, "He stretched out his arms on the hard wood of the cross that everyone might come within the reach of his saving embrace." *Amen.*

(Editor's note: This sermon was preached by Fr. David on September 11, 2015 at St. Paul's Chapel of Trinity Episcopal Church Wall Street, directly across from the World Trade Center. The chapel became instantly recognized as the "the little chapel that stood," providing the ministry of healing and service for the eight-month recovery effort after 9/11. Fr. David is currently serving as vicar at the parish of St. Joan of Arc in Pflugerville, Texas).

Reconciliation

Rev. George McGavern

I was at a conference where someone was speaking on the topic of racial reconciliation. The presenter asked the audience, given our country's history of slavery, emancipation, Jim Crow, the legal doctrine of "separate but equal," and ongoing racism, "Has there ever been a time when we were *conciled*?" In other words, reconciliation anticipates a time when parties to an estrangement were not estranged or separated or divided. The rhetorical question had its intended effect. It was a powerful question for reflection and called the group to look deeply into the work that needed to be done. However, it missed the point about reconciliation altogether.

There was a time when we were *conciled*, and that time was in the Garden of Eden. There is something very important about the story of creation in Genesis. The story emphasizes a central and important idea: what God creates is good and what God created in humanity, he created to be in relationship. The goodness of creation is marked by partnership and relationship: humanity, in good and pleasing relationship with the earth, with all creation, with one another, and with God.

Adam and Eve's disobedience, an archetype of the human condition, had disastrous consequences. The ground produced thorns and thistles. Animals died and humanity was clothed in their hides. Relationships were broken between us and the earth, us and creatures, us and God, and us and one another. The whole of human history continues from there and looks much like it does today—pollution, poaching, domination, slavery, misogyny, violence, godlessness, war, and oppression.

In a world where power stops at nothing to further its increase, where economic and political forces drive expansion and conquest, where there is oppression, where freedom is stifled, and where ethnic scapegoating propels a narrative of violence, war exists. Terrorism and Nazism notwithstanding, the crises in Rwanda, Darfur, Somalia, Uganda, and other places throughout the modern world give rise to the question: "At what point does a violent response become justifiable over a passive response?" There is this notion of a "just war," a violent and devastating action being justified so long as certain criteria are met. Yet is there justice? War is tragic even when it is necessary. War is sin even when it is justified.

Pope John Paul II often said war is the defeat of humanity. While he recognized just causes to take up arms (most notably in honoring his own country's resistance to Hitler), he maintained that even just wars are defeats for humanity and that they do not generally solve the problems they are fought for and that they prove ultimately futile. What is acknowledged by this claim is the recognition that the reality which produces a necessary and just response of violence is itself a failure worthy of guilt and repentance. Furthermore, even when violence does resolve the situation that justified it to begin with, it is never sufficient in and of itself. The issues which precipitated the violence will persist beyond it and even become exacerbated by deep-seated hatred and resentment. This is where the work of reconciliation comes in—not trying to go back to some time when Nazis and Jews got along, but striving to be in the rightness of relationship that we were created for even though we were born into a life of brokenness.

When the Christian church talks about God's ministry of reconciliation in the world, it is referring to God dealing with the brokenness of the world—the very brokenness that produces war—and restoring good and right relationships. Mother Teresa reduced all the world's suffering and brokenness to a single root cause "If we have no peace," she said, "it is because we have forgotten that we belong to each other."

Reconciliation is the work of confessing the ways in which we have embodied this forgotten kinship, accepting the forgiveness for the hurt we have caused and striving to respect the dignity of every human being. It is not about justifying the actions that we took, whether we had to or not, but about owning how our actions caused injury to one another and to ourselves. When we hurt one another, we ourselves are wounded too. If I kill a man who breaks into my home and is a threat to my family, I am justified. Yet the action of killing someone to whom I belong (whether I like it or not) has wounded me morally. The justification tries its best not to allow me to acknowledge the sin, and that is when justification becomes dangerous.

My cousin, Tom, served as an airborne ranger in the conflict in Panama, and with the 1st Infantry Mechanized Division in operation Desert Storm. Both conflicts were very violent in terms of his action. However, the conflict that eventually overcame him and took his life was Panama. A position he was ordered to defend was infiltrated by children with rifles, some as young as 10 years old. To protect the lives of his unit, he and his brothers had to gun down these children. He told this story to a Vietnam veteran shortly before he died. Tom aimed and fired his rifle through tears while shouting, "I'm sorry! I'm sorry! I'm sorry!" On the night he died, he was reliving this moment, firing an imaginary rifle while running through his neighborhood screaming, "I'm sorry! I'm sorry! I'm sorry!" When he was restrained by police, his heart gave out because of the amount of cocaine in his system.

When Tom got out of the army and came home, the world had no room for his story. If he had not killed those children, he and others would have died. He was *justified*, so he was not free to share his feelings of guilt with his family. His church was not a safe place to acknowledge the horrors he endured and take responsibility for what he did. *Justification* offers no healing. Even sharing his story with a Vietnam veteran who himself was dealing with PTSD was not enough to alleviate the pain. Finding understanding is not always enough.

The Christian language of confession, repentance, and forgiveness acknowledges the brokenness of humanity, our role in hurting others, and the truth of God's forgiveness. Here is the central truth of the cross in Christianity. It was not God's will that Jesus should be crucified and killed. It was the world's will. It was our will. And Jesus submitted to that will perfectly. The world was judged when it put its source of light and life to death on the cross. Yet even from the cross, Jesus cried, "Forgive them, Father." These were not idle words. God in Jesus descended to the darkest depths of humanity, and when he rose up, he raised all humanity up with him. This is God's work of reconciliation in the world.

War is a failure of humanity, and it was for this failure that God came to bring forgiveness and to remind us that we belong to one another. Confession, forgiveness, and amendment of life. We, the church, need to be certain we are open to hear the stories of our veterans, to listen to what they are feeling and experiencing, to acknowledge the moral injury they have suffered, and to offer forgiveness. Forgiveness not because the war was justified or their actions were justified or any other reason that can make us feel better about it. Forgiveness because war is tragic and it is sin and absolutely no one is outside of the reach of God's loving embrace. Nothing is beyond God's compassion.

Just as we, the church, need to listen to our veterans, we need to call those who stayed home into repentance, too, to make us a part of the reconciliation. Reconciliation for the soldier is not enough. Those of us who stayed home while others went to fight the wars we justified are in as much need of reconciliation as the soldier. For no one is righteous, not one. I am in need of confessing my own acceptance of war, my unwillingness to put myself in harm's way, and my desire to protect my life and my way of life. God forgive me.

My cousin, Tom, was not able to tell anyone in Panama he was sorry even though he tried through his screams. I could have told him I was sorry, but I did not. Maybe the most important part of reconciliation for a soldier is when he or she can hear us say "I'm sorry" to them. If I could just own up to my own role in the war and apologize to our veterans for having asked them to suffer dreadful horrors on my behalf, maybe then my kinship with them in their suffering could be made real. A veteran once told me, "I can believe in God's forgiveness, but I just cannot forgive myself." Maybe the first step for a veteran of war to forgive himself or herself is to forgive us for asking them to go in the first place. Maybe. Just maybe "I'm sorry" goes a lot further than "Thank you for your service."

If the church cannot call its community to repentance, then wars will never cease. There is a day when wars will cease. The only time when wars did not exist was for that brief period in the Garden of Eden. God's ministry of reconciliation is putting all the hurt to right, and one day we will cherish the peace that comes from this one simple truth: we belong to one another.

(Editor's note: The Rev. George McGavern is currently the rector at Episcopal Church of the Good Shepherd in Tomball, Texas)

Helpful Organizations, Websites, and Reference Materials

Below you will find a number of resources for military and veteran families. There are resources for children, parents, educators, and providers. These listings are not endorsements, but are provided for their informational value. Please click on the type of resource you are interested in exploring.

Books

For veterans or service members (and adult family members)

Armstrong, Keith, Best, Suzanne, and Domenici, Paula. *Courage After Fire: Coping Strategies for Returning Soldiers and Their Families.* New York: Ulysses Press, 2006.

Cantrell, Bridget, and Dean, Chuck. *Down Range: To Iraq and Back.* Washington: Pine Hill Graphics, 2005.

Matsakis, Aphrodite. *Back from the Front: Combat Trauma, Love, and the Family.* Maryland: Sidran Press, 2007.

Matsakis, Aphrodite. *Trust After Trauma: A Guide to Relationships for Survivors and Those Who Love Them.* Oakland: New Harbinger Publications, 1998.

Henderson, Kristin. *While They're at War: The True Story of American Families on the Homefront.* Massachusetts: Houghton Mifflin Harcourt Publishing, 2006.

Peters, David. *Post-Traumatic God: How the Church Cares for People Who Have Been to Hell and Back.* Pennsylvania: Morehouse Publishing, 2016.

Slone, Lori, and Friedman, Matthew. *After the war zone: A practical Guide for Returning Troops and Their Families.* Massachusetts: Da Capo Press, 2008.

For kids

Andrews, Beth. *I Miss You! A Military Kid's Book About Deployment.* Maryland: Prometheus Books, 2007.

Bunting, Eve. *My Red Balloon.* New York: Boyd Mills Publishing, 2005.

Ferguson-Cohen, Michelle. *Daddy, You're My Hero!* Ohio: Little Redhaired Girl Publishing, 2005.

Jensen-Fritz, Sara, Jones-Johnson, Paula, and Zitzow, Thea L. *You and Your Military Hero: Building Positive Thinking Skills During Your Hero's Deployment.* Bookhouse Fulfillment Publishing, 2009.

Sherman, Michelle D. and Sherman, DeAnne M. *Finding My Way: A Teen's Guide to Living with a Parent Who Has Experienced Trauma.* Texas: Seeds of Hope Books, 2005. (available at www.seedsofhopebooks.com).

Sportelli-Rehak, Angela. *Uncle Sam's Kids in When Duty Calls.* New Jersey: Abidenme Books Publishing, 2003.

Timperley, Geri, and Arro, Nikki. *A Very Long Time.* Pennsylvania: Igi Publ, 2005.

Websites

Emotional health

Innovations, MindWise. Help Yourself. Help Others. http://www.militarymentalhealth.org/.
Mental Health America. "MHA." http://www.nmha.org/.
PTSD, National Center for. "VA.gov: Veterans Affairs." Home, August 15, 2013. http://www.ptsd.va.gov/.
Sherman, Michelle D. "An 18-Session Curriculum for People Who Care about Someone Who Has a Mental Illness." Support and Family Education: Mental Health Facts for Families, April 2008. http://www.ouhsc.edu/safeprogram.

For parents and educators

Child Care Aware® of America. "Homepage." https://www.childcareaware.org/.
The National Child Traumatic Stress Network. "Homepage." https://www.nctsn.org/?pid=ctr_top_military.
Military Child Education Coalition MCEC. "Military Child Education Coalition: MCEC." https://www.military-child.org/.
Welcome Back Parenting: "A Guide for Reconnecting Families after Military Deployment." http://www.welcome-backparenting.org.

Deployment

Jacobson, S. and Colon, E. *Coming Home: What to Expect, How to Deal When You Return from Combat*. Military OneSource, 2008. (Comic booklet available from Military OneSource.)

Sander, A. "Picking up the Pieces after TBI: A Guide for Family Members." 2002. https://www.lapublishing.com/blog/wp-content/uploads/2009/08/TIRR-Picking-up-the-pieces.pdf

"Resources for Military and Veteran Families." https://www.mghpact.org/for-parents/other-resources/for-military-and-veteran-families?fontsize=5

"Surviving Deployment: Information and Resources for Military Families. http://www.survivingdeployment.com

Rand Corporation. "Post-Deployment Stress: What Families Should Know, What Families Can Do." 2008. https://www.rand.org/content/dam/rand/pubs/corporate_pubs/2008/RAND_CP534-2008-03.pdf

Rand Corporation. "Post-Deployment Stress: What You Should Know, What You Can Do." 2008. https://www.rand.org/content/dam/rand/pubs/corporate_pubs/2008/RAND_CP534-2008-03.pdf

General support and resources

- Military One Source (toll-free 1-800-342-9647). https://www.militaryonesource.mil/national-guard/joint-services-support-program
- Benefits fact sheets, US Department of Veterans Affairs. https://benefits.va.gov/BENEFITS/factsheets.asp
- Returning service members (OEF/OIF), https://www.oefoif.va.gov/.
- Vet centers information and vet Centers by state: https://www.veteranownedbusiness.com/state-vet-

center-list.php. Vet Center staff are available toll-free and around the clock at 877-WAR-VETS (927-8387).
- National Resource Directory—Online tool for wounded, ill, and injured troops, veterans, and their families, providing access to more than 11,000 services and resources at the national, state, and local levels. https://nrd.gov

Videos

"Treating the Invisible Wounds of War and ICARE: What Primary Care Providers Need to Know about Mental Health Issues Facing Returning Service Members and Their Families." Operation Military Kids, April 18, 2019. https://www.operationmilitarykids.org/somk.

"Young Children on the Homefront." ZERO TO THREE. https://www.zerotothree.org/parenting/military-and-veteran-families-support.

"Young Heroes: Military Deployment Through the Eyes of Youth." Operation Military Kids, April 18, 2019. https://www.operationmilitarykids.org/somk.

Support Organizations

- **The Birdwell Foundation**—The Birdwell Foundation's volunteers and counselors can help those suffering from PTSD symptoms brought on by TBI. Their outreach is designed for families, veterans, and first responders. Available in multilocation across the US. (PO Box 690748, Houston TX 77069, office

phone 210-486-1639, *in crisis, call* **(830) 822-2563**. (www.birdwellfoundation.org, 888-316-0123)
- **Grief Recovery Institute**—An internationally recognized authority on grief recovery, offers training programs. (www.griefrecoverymethod.com, 800-344-7606)
- **GriefNet**—Internet community of persons dealing with grief, death, and major loss. (www.griefnet.org, PO Box 3272, Ann Arbor, MI 48106-3272, cendra@griefnet.org)
- **KinderMourn**—In addition to serving the special needs of bereaved parents, this organization assists children grieving the death of a family member or friend. (www.kindermourn.org, 704-376-2580)
- **The Compassionate Friends**—This support organization is designed to assist families in grief resolution following the death of a child. (www.compassionate-friends.org, 630-990-0010)
- **Lone Survivor Foundation**—Lone Survivor Foundation restores, empowers, and renews hope for wounded service members, veterans, and their families through health, wellness, and therapeutic support. It is our mission to guide veterans and their families toward a path of healing from combat trauma through a series of no cost post-traumatic growth programs. A copy of DD214 and referral from a physician or mental health provider are required to begin the application process. (1414 11th St., Huntsville TX 77340, 936-755-6075, info@lonesurvivorfoundation.org)
- **The Mighty Oaks Foundation**—The Mighty Oaks Foundation provides faith and peer-based discipleship through a series of programs, outpost meetings, and speaking events. The Mighty Oaks Warrior Programs

hosts such men, women, and marriage advance programs at multiple locations nationwide. The warriors who attend are fully sponsored for training, meals, and lodging needs to ensure that upon arrival to the ranch, each warrior is focused solely on his or her recovery and identifying his or her purpose in moving forward. (29910 Murietta Hot Springs Rd., Ste. G530, Murietta, CA 92563, info@mightyoaksprograms.org)

- **The Semper Fi Fund**—They provide urgently needed resources and support for combat-wounded, critically ill, and catastrophically injured members of the US Armed Forces and their families from injury through recovery. Assistance is provided to help wounded veterans assimilate back into their communities. Integrative wellness programs provide holistic health therapies to service members. (www.semperfifund.org, 760-725-3680)
- **Travis Manion Foundation (TMF)**—This foundation empowers veterans and families of fallen heroes to develop character in future generations. In 2007, First Lieutenant Travis Manion (USMC) was killed in Iraq while saving his wounded teammates. Today, Travis's legacy lives on in the words he spoke before leaving for his final deployment, "If not me, then who…" Guided by this mantra, veterans continue their service, develop strong relationships with their communities, and thrive in their postmilitary lives. As a result, communities prosper and the character of our nation's heroes live on in the next generation. This foundation appears in multiple locations across the US. (TMF Headquarters, PO Box 1485, Doylestown, PA 18901, 215.348.9080)

- **Starfish Foundation/Healing Warrior Hearts**—We help veterans and trauma survivors heal and find their joy again! Healing Warrior Hearts provides retreats in Texas and Wisconsin for veterans and their families, dedicated to healing the emotional, moral, and spiritual wounds of military service. Texas for Heroes and Starfish Foundation (WI), 501c3 charitable organizations, sponsor Healing Warrior Hearts weekend retreats at no cost to veterans and their families. These are all volunteer organizations; retreats are staffed by veterans and civilians who witness participants' stories and welcome them into community with unconditional regard and respect. (www.healingwarriorhearts.org 800-236-4692 or 414-374-5433. Mailing Address: 2437 N. Booth St., Milwaukee, WI 53212 Conference Center: 10919 W. Bluemound Ave #50, Wauwatosa, WI 53226)
- **The 10-33 Foundation**—provides crisis intervention for veterans and their families through education and crisis intervention services. All intervention services are peer and professional based. Crisis services available via multiple platforms. For more information email: info@1033foundation.org https://www.1033foundation.org Find us on Facebook at: 10-33 Foundation
- **Freedom Equine Connection**—a division of The 10-33 Foundation Freedom Equine Connection facilitates the opportunity for healing through experiential, ground based, solution-oriented therapy. Equine Assisted Psychotherapy and Learning is an increasingly popular method of treating addictions, trauma, PTSD, behavioral disorders, depression, and more.

Office phone 707-249-5819, https://www.1033foundation.org/equine-therapy Find us on Facebook at: Freedom Equine Connection. Our program is located in Northern California, for a program near you, visit Eagala.org

Description/Meaning of our logo:

The **Blue Ring** symbolizes Warriors Peace, Truth and Tranquility.

The **White Background** symbolizes Warriors Light and Purity.

The **Hands Shaking** symbolizes Warriors Comradery.

Thr **Cross** symbolizes Warriors Hope for Tomorrow.

The **Angel Wings** symbolizes Warriors Protective Spirit.

The **Shield** symbolizes Warriors Armor.

The **Red** symbolizes the Bloodshed by previous Warriors.

Chuck Wright

NOTES

About the Author

Charles "Chuck" Wright

Born in Memphis, Tennessee, Charles spent his childhood years in Tennessee, Mississippi, South Carolina, Missouri, and Oklahoma. Being married for only a year and just graduated from Southwest Baptist College, Charles volunteered for the United States Marines during the Vietnam War.

After six months of jungle training in Hawaii, he was sent to Vietnam as a replacement for the Third Battalion, 4th Marines, a line battalion along the DMZ, and soon became a battalion courier. After his tour of duty in Vietnam, he was honorably discharged as a sergeant. Charles returned to Oklahoma to complete college at Oklahoma State University.

Charles has two sons—Sean, and his wife, Betsy, with their four children residing in Nashville, Tennessee. Charles's other son, Tobin, and his wife, Khryste, with their three children reside in Katy, Texas.

About the Co-Editor

Richard Dorn, co-editor, serves as an advisor to the Board of STP Warriors. He worked in various capacities in the chemical and petrochemical industries until his retirement. He was a commissioned officer, serving as an infantry platoon leader in the Vietnam War. After Vietnam, he continued in the Army reserve until his retirement.

CPSIA information can be obtained
at www.ICGtesting.com
Printed in the USA
LVHW031334020921
696729LV00001B/2